Hire Me!

Hire Me!

Successful Interviewing Techniques

Calvin Lovick & Angela M. Cranon-Charles, M.A.

 iUniverse®

HIRE ME!
SUCCESSFUL INTERVIEWING TECHNIQUES

iUniverse books may be ordered through booksellers or by contacting:

iUniverse
1663 Liberty Drive
Bloomington, IN 47403
www.iuniverse.com
1-800-Authors (1-800-288-4677)

ISBN: 978-1-5320-3763-4 (sc)
ISBN: 978-1-5320-3762-7 (e)

Library of Congress Control Number: 2017917890

Print information available on the last page.

iUniverse rev. date: 05/26/2018

INTRODUCTION

Unemployed, underemployed, or have a desire for a career change? In today's economy it is a reality that many have settled for a job they don't like, or have been unemployed for years. This could all change, if you are equipped with the right tools...and in this case...the right information to GET A JOB.

But what you may not know are the best ways *to actually find a job* in today's market.

And that's where this book can help.

Hire Me! arms job seekers with the necessary tools to successfully navigate the tricky job market that is extremely challenging in today's economic climate. This book provides strategies that, when followed, should make finding a job less stressful. Most importantly, it contains tips which should make finding a job a reality.

Hire Me! is an easy read that is filled with virtually everything job seekers need to know, from how to make their resumes informative, attractive, and engaging to how to conduct themselves during lunch or dinner job interviews – and everything in between.

This book also provides sage advice for people already employed, including what lines not to cross in professional relationships, how to best ask for a raise, knowing what interviewing techniques to follow, and much, much more.

So, if you're among the millions of people trying to land a job these days, or if you want to obtain a better job than the one you have, *Hire Me!* has something for you.

Remember: There's no harm in not knowing something. The harm comes when you don't try to learn what you need to know.

And when it comes to the job market, savvy publishers Los Angeles Businessman Calvin Lovick and Award-Winning Journalist and Professor Angela M. Cranon-Charles, M.A. have created the book of the century. Together they have more than 50 years of experience in the employment industry and as publishers.

CONTENTS

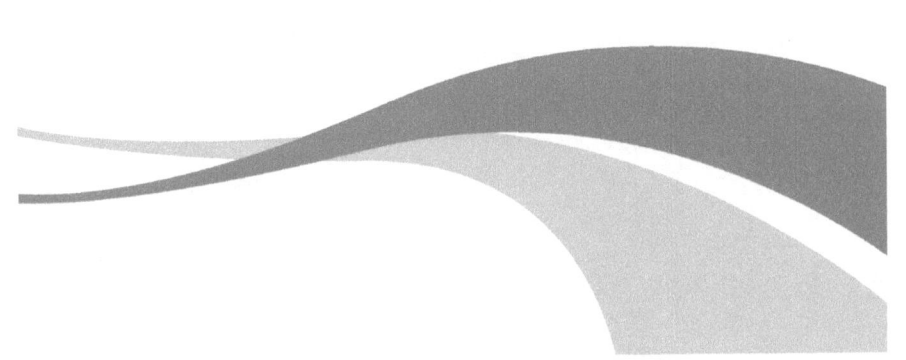

PART 1

CREATE A WINNING RESUME

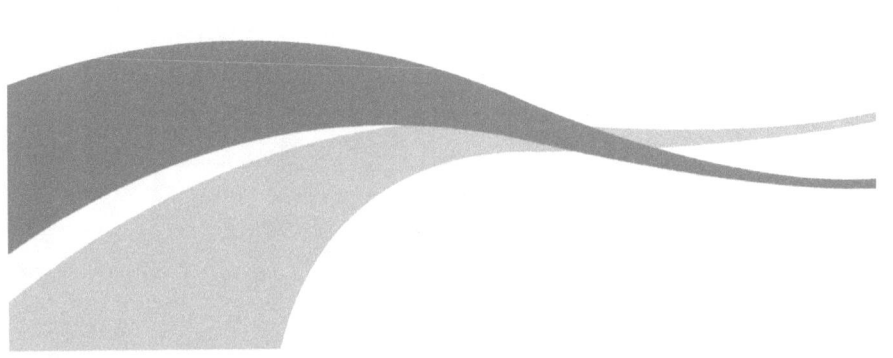

CHAPTER 1

Don't Lie on Your Resume

Don't Lie on Your Resume

Unfortunately, people have been lying on resumes for decades, but only the high-profile cases are revealed.

When a national job-research company, ResumeDoctor.com, fact-checked some 1,000 resumes in its database, it discovered that nearly 43 percent of job applicants, in one way or another, distorted their past. Why? Evidently, people think that everyone else is doing it, so they might as well do it, too. They are trying to get a job, so we can blame their behavior on fierce competition in a tight employment market - and the mistaken notion that little white lies will do no harm. That couldn't be more wrong, considering how often people get caught.

Plus, something you put on your resume today could haunt you years later. Look at what happened to RadioShack CEO David Edmondson - make that former CEO. Edmondson joined RadioShack in 1994 and was a senior executive since late 1998, serving as senior vice president and chief operating officer with a $6 million salary. Eventually, the truth about his qualifications leaked out when a Fort Worth newspaper identified false information on his resume. Edmondson had claimed that he had received degrees in theology and psychology from Pacific Coast Baptist College in California, which moved in 1998 to Oklahoma and renamed itself Heartland Baptist Bible College. But the school had no records of the degrees. Edmondson admitted the information was incorrect, and lost his job because of a lie on his resume more than a decade previous.

Deception on resumes is a common mistake. Remember George O'Leary? He was Notre Dame's football coach - for all of five days, before the lies on his resume caught up with him. He had said he had a master's degree in education from "NYU-Stony Brook University" - a campus that doesn't exist. The message to you is: don't lie on your resume. Watch out, because companies are cracking down and doing more resume-checking than ever before. Increasingly, they're also scrutinizing criminal records, credit reports and even driving records.

There's greater attention and sensitivity about background checks. Publicly traded companies, in particular, are under pressure to check up on people - because of the Sarbanes-Oxley law on reporting requirements. The most frequent fibs are about dates of employment, job titles, and education. The ResumeDoctor.com study found that people said they stayed at jobs longer than they really did. Some are trying to match the requirements in a job posting when they don't have enough years of experience.

Don't lie to cover up long periods of joblessness - and there's no need to do so. In today's economy, there's no shame in losing your job. Twenty years ago, there was a stigma about being laid off; now, it's the norm.

Don't inflate job titles in hopes of qualifying for a higher position - and higher pay - than you currently have. If you took on tasks that higher-ups were supposed to do, you can say so on your resume. But, don't pretend you had the job title to match the extra responsibilities.

Don't say you earned degrees when you were actually a couple of semesters short, or say you graduated from a school that you never attended. The career consequences can be deadly. If you get caught lying, you won't get the job you apply for - and you might make yourself an untouchable in your industry, wearing a life-long scarlet letter on your chest.

Be truthful and explain your circumstances, instead of getting caught in a lie later on down the road that could impact your current job and certainly any future ones.

CHAPTER 2

Resume Checklist

Resume Checklist

When writing a resume, as simple as it may seem, there are a few rules to follow that could mean all the difference between being reviewed or being filed, in the worse place ever (the trash). So, before you actually sit down to create, spruce up, or reinvent your resume, pay attention to these few simple guidelines that could land you a job:

Golden rule is to avoid personal pronouns.

Personal pronouns, such as I, me, or my, get in the way of a smooth read. Take yourself out of the equation in the first and second person. The reader does not question who wrote the resume, so there is no need to insert these words that even get a thumbs-down when writing scholarly material.

Action verbs keep the resume moving.

Action verbs give your resume that certain movement of progress and direction from one point to the next, particularly when using bullet points for your professional experience lists.

Avoid using "filler" words.

Resumes should shine like diamonds. The bling of your resume should be evident. Fluffy and extra use of the same words will slow down the read of your resume and stand in the way of the bling that should be shining throughout. Don't use extra words or repeat some of the same words. Keep your resume moving.

Key elements needed in a resume.

Make sure your resume has solid information, i.e., education, professional summary, professional experience, key dates and brief accomplishment lists, technical skills, and references.

Choose your words carefully.

Look at the qualifications for the job, and use some of the same words throughout your resume to describe and list your experiences. Sometimes resumes are put through a computerized system to recognize key words. If your resume does not contain the key words, it will be rejected.

Order does matter.

As you play the match word game, also put those qualifications at the top of your description, so that the reader or computer will recognize the key words immediately.

No Nonsense.

Make sure your information is relevant on the resume. Even though you may have done other work, if those accomplishments are not relevant to the immediate position you are applying to, avoid putting it directly on the resume, or create the description to match what the employer is looking for. Put the irrelevant work experience in your curriculum vitae or mention it in your interview, if you can make it relevant to the job you are seeking.

Easy on the eye lists.

Be sure to list responsibilities using bullet points, but don't make your resume look like a grocery item checklist. Check for quantifying information. However, your lists of experiences need to be solid. Make sure you answer the questions of how many, how much, how frequent, and so forth.

Meet the challenges.

Resumes should meet the challenges of the job you are seeking. Be specific with your bullet point lists. Let the reader know the challenges met.

Too specific or too general?

Generalizing a resume and your experience will not get you the job. It tells the employer that you did a little bit of this and a little bit of that. If that is not the case, be specific while being relevant. Tailor your specific skills and job experience to the employer's needs.

Page numbers do count.

When an application specifies page count, stick to it. Spending more pages does not impress the employer, but tells them that you do not know how to follow instructions. Impress them with your ability to give them what they want.

Objectives should match.

Create a strong objective that is specific to the job. Never use a generic objective statement. Each resume submission should reflect the specific objectives of the job being sought.

Creative?

Designs on the cover letter or within the resume may not be suitable for all careers. An artist or graphic designer, for example, may get away with some designs to show off creativity, but this is not the norm. Keep the resume crisp and clean-looking. Avoid designs unless the type of job calls for it.

Proofread

Sometimes mistakes are missed, but for the most part, it is essential to proofread all work. Not only does spelling count, but so too does grammar. If you can't do it, let someone else look for your potential mistakes. Too many will surely eliminate you in the race for a new job.

Contact information.

Make sure employers are not searching for your contact information, i.e., name, phone numbers, fax, and email addresses. Avoid putting your Facebook, Twitter or any other social media account, unless it leads the employer to more attributes that make you shine. Otherwise, don't bother.

Triple-check.

Triple check everything before pushing that submit button. If you are unable to edit your submissions, then your final push of a button could mean a new job or a rejection letter. Step back from reading your resume for a few hours until your eyes and brain are clear. Then approach the document with fresh eyes or, better yet, let someone else read it.

CHAPTER 3

Resume Writing

Resume Writing

The purpose of the resume is to get the interview; therefore, it is critical to develop a resume that makes you stand out from the crowd. The resume is a summary of your qualifications and experiences used in the job search campaign. It must be pleasing to the eye so the reader is enticed to pick it up and read it. It "wets the appetite", and stimulates interest in meeting and learning more about you. It inspires the prospective employer to pick up the phone and ask you to come in for an interview. A good resume is essential for your job search for a number of reasons:

Organizes your qualifications and past experiences to support your objective

Provides a good document to leave behind so the prospective employer knows who you are

May occasionally open doors in networking and contacts

Resume writing has changed during the past decades. There are two basic kinds of resumes:

Chronological

Functional

The chronological resume lists your skills and accomplishments in reverse chronological order, with most recent experience first. The functional resume lists your accomplishments by various function, e.g., marketing, finance, and human resources.

In the past, chronological resumes were preferred. However, because of the fluctuating economy, with so many mergers and acquisitions, people are now changing jobs more frequently. Therefore, the "functional" resume should be used to minimize the appearance that you have been job-hopping.

Resumes should be one to two pages in length. Job seekers with less than 10 years of experience should be able to condense their resume into one page. More experienced job seekers with more than 10 years of experience should have a two-page resume.

CHRONOLOGICAL RESUME

This resume places emphasis on recent experience and indicates a progression in responsibility.

Advantages	Disadvantages
Emphasizes career growth	Highlights spotty work history
Emphasizes growth in responsibilities	Not appropriate if changing careers
Emphasizes impressive job titles	

FUNCTIONAL RESUME

This resume allows you to highlight major areas of accomplishments, strengths, and abilities. The areas are then organized in order of importance according to your current career objectives.

Advantages	**Disadvantages**
Emphasizes skills	De-emphasizes job growth
Emphasizes wide variety of experience	De-emphasizes managerial/ supervisory
Masks any spotty work history	Disliked in engineering and business

ACTION WORDS USED TO DESCRIBE ACCOMPLISHMENTS

accomplished	activated	built
adjusted	calculated	coordinated
advertised	compiled	defined
advised	constructed	designed
analyzed	created	devised
arranged	drafted	executed
assembled	edited	explained
assisted	enlarged	illustrated
calculated	established	implemented
catalogued	evaluated	initiated
chaired	examined	innovated
collaborated	expanded	integrated
conceptualized	expedited	interviewed
conciliated	fabricated	investigated

conducted	facilitated	maintained
consulted	familiarized	manipulated
contracted	formulated	marketed
coordinated	generated	modified
delegated	governed	monitored
demonstrated	guided	negotiated
devised	hired	obtained
directed	identified	persuaded
distributed	improved	presented
effected	increased	presided
explained	indexed	proposed
managed	informed	publicized
motivated	instrumental	recommended
organized	invented	recorded
programmed	prepared	recruited
promoted	programmed	related
simulated	revised	surveyed
supervised	specified	synthesized
taught	used	transmitted

Examples of Accomplishments

Accomplishments are work-related outcomes of your work that you feel good about, such as: you did it or you helped do it, you received satisfaction from doing it, you were proud of it, and you did it well. The following is a list of sample work-related accomplishments:

- Achieved the highest production schedule in the department
- Worked the past two years with perfect attendance

- Made the least amount of errors in the department
- Selected to take part in the Quality Control Committee
- Won the safety slogan contest
- Received cash award for suggestions program
- Successfully managed a budget with annual expenditure of over $300,000
- Demonstrated machines and production processes to customers
- Successfully opened profitable foreign markets
- Salvaged a previously unprofitable operation

Research shows that only one interview is granted for every 200 resumes received by the average employer. Research also tells us that your resume will be quickly scanned rather than read. Ten to twenty seconds is all the time you have to persuade a prospective employer to read further. What this means is the decision to interview a candidate is usually based on an overall first impression of the resume, and a quick screening which impresses the reader and convinces them to grant an interview.

As a result, the top half of the first page of your resume will either make or break you. When writing a resume, some job seekers choose to state an objective on their resume, rather than including it in the body of their cover letter. Stating an objective can convince employers that you know what you want to do and are familiar with the field. While stating your objective on your resume is optional, having an objective for your resume is not - you need to be clear about your employment goals.

By the time the employer reads the first few lines, you have either caught that person's interest or your resume has failed. That is the reason your resume is an advertising tool. You hope it will have the same result as a well-written ad-to get the reader to respond.

CHAPTER 4

How to Build a
Strong Resume

How to Build a Strong Resume

Avoid padding your resume with untruths. Instead, learn how to enhance it with what was learned on the job.

Recent College Graduates:

Although recent college graduates have little to no professional experience, a resume is necessary to land a job. A lack of experience does not necessarily make your resume appear to be insufficient or unimpressive; however, your resume does depend on the detailed job descriptions of your experience to impress an interviewer. For example, if you worked as a cashier or at a fast-food outlet at minimum wage, it is essential to focus more on the skills learned and demonstrated than the title of your position. Your resume can list the following skills:

- Strong people skills
- Ability to make impromptu decisions
- Ability to multi-task
- Followed instructions
- Worked closely with management
- Demonstrated the willingness to assist
- Responsible for managing daily cash
- Responsible for opening and closing
- Reliable

Remember, a resume does not represent only history of employment, but it is an opportunity to showcase specific skills that employers are looking for in a potential candidate to hire, especially those with degrees.

Also, be sure to look at the job details, and the qualifications for the job you are seeking, in order to match your skills as closely as possible with the employer's.

- Make sure the resume is easy to read. Look at professional examples.

- Avoid making the style fancy or too creative-looking when applying for most, but not all, positions. Of course, if you are applying for a job that requires creativity that would be different.
- Print with black ink.
- Use high-quality heavy stock paper.
- Be consistent with font size - If subheadings are 12 font and bullets are 11, keep it that way the entire resume.
- Have someone proofread the resume before submitting it.

Experienced Candidates:

Unlike with recent college graduates, job titles and experience are important to showcase if you have been in the workplace for years. Employers want to see if you have held high-powered positions or handled management duties that would easily take you to the next step up the ladder. Therefore, it is essential to match your skills with what is being required by the employer you are targeting. Make sure your resume reflects "solid" experience and skills, and, sometimes, it is necessary to be very specific about a task performed on the job. However, remember the employer is not looking to read a novel, so be very specific and focused on what you put on your resume.

Also, remember that every professional needs more than one resume. Each time you seek a job you might need to revamp your existing one, and include only what the employer is looking for on the one you submit. Of course, include a few additional skills so that the employer will notice you not only have skills they are looking for, but additional abilities and experiences as well.

Use the resume to outline your titles and experience, but use a Curriculum Vitae (CV) to expand on your years of achievements. Known as a CV, most employers want the more experienced job seeker to have one. This comprises a detailed account of your job duties, outside activities that enhance your skills, and demonstrated leadership talents.

For example, if you not only managed a department, but also held workshops to improve employee skills, unified the department, or accomplished goals, reveal that in your CV. Presentations given, volunteer service performed, work-related or skill-related seminars attended, and any other activity that you were involved in that gives the employer a broader review of your abilities, performance, dedication and leadership skills, put these in the CV. List hobbies. Your future employer might find interest in you because he/she also enjoys the same activities. Like the resume, the CV should not exceed one or two pages; one is always preferred.

Whether you are a recent college graduate, newly skilled talent, or carry years of experience, do not fear searching for the job of your dreams. Just remember that your resume is 'your first impression'. If you are a go-getter, let the resume reflect that. If you are a leader person, let the resume showcase this. If you are a multi-tasker, let that piece of paper give the same impression. A solid resume and Curriculum Vitae will help to get you in the door before even meeting the interviewer.

Resume:

- Objective
- Education - Institution, dates, concentration
- Experience Summary
- Job history - Include titles, dates, responsibilities
- Work-related skills - computer, specific machinery, etc.

Also, search websites to write the perfect resume that suits your particular career search:

Key terms to search:

- How to write a resume.
- How to write a resume for _____ (name your specific field of interest).
- Resume writing.
- Simple resume writing.
- Tools to write a resume.
- Resume builder.

Sample Resume:

Name
Email:

**11111 Curry Street, Los Angeles, Ca. 90000   (310) 293-3333 (phone)/
(562) 926-0000 (fax)**

**OBJECTIVE: To work as a reporter for a magazine that has domestic
and international exposure.**

EDUCATION

- Master of Arts Degree in Political Science
- Bachelor of Arts in Journalism
- Professional Designation Broadcast Certificate

- Harvard Academy, New York, NY (HA-1997)
- San Marcos University, Warren, MI (SMU-1982)
- University of Kani, Los Angeles, L.A., CA (UK-1991)

PROFESSIONAL EXPERIENCE SUMMARY:

Award-winning **Journalist since 1982 has extensive experience** in
hosting, writing/reporting of general assignments, including business,
features, hard-news, and profiles. Solid media background also includes
anchoring, managing a news department, developing programs,
producing newscasts, public affairs shows, debates and forums for ABC
network and cable stations. owner of Hollywood Scriptwriter Magazine.

30-year Public Relations specialist, which includes publishing and
designing newsletters, writing press releases, writing and designing
brochures, press kits, and internal/external literature, coordinating
and implementing unique marketing and community promotions and
internal/external event activities.

16-year Professor online and on-ground, college level. Responsible for
teaching a variety of subjects, which include Political Science, Film,

English, Oral Communications, Public Speaking, History, Written Communications, Government, and Team-building.

Journalism/Public Relations Employment Summary:

- ***Hollywood Scriptwriter Magazine***, an international trade publication that profiles TV screenwriters, producers and directors 2003 - Present (*www.hollywoodscriptwriter.com*)
  - Owner and Editor-in-Chief
  - Layout and design publication (50 to 80 pages)
  - Publish newsletters and brochures
  - Manage staff and daily operation of business
  - Design and manage website

- **Lovick Career Journal Magazine** -
  1990 - Present (www.lovickdiversitycareer.com)
  - Associate Publisher and Editor-in-Chief
  - Editor and writer
  - Public relations and marketing specialist

- *Uniform Airport* – Manager, Public Relations and Television Host - 1995 - 2000
  - Produced and designed monthly airport newsletter and specialty brochure
  - Served as editor, writer, and photographer for newsletter and press releases
  - Managed Public Relations Tour Guide Staff
  - Media Relations
  - Hosted weekly 30-minute talk show "Plane Facts"

Related Journalism/Public Relations Experience:

- Community Newspaper "Freelance" Reporter
- Golden Academy – Public Relations/Faculty Instructor (contract)/ Marketing
- Continental Cablevision, Calif. - News Director/Exec. Prod./GA Reporter

- Financial News Network, Calif. - Producer/Writer
- KAMC - Channel 28 (ABC), Texas - GA Reporter
- KVOP AM/KATX FM, Texas - News Director/Reporter/Talk Show Host
- So. CA Publishing Newspaper, Calif. - GA Reporter/Editor
- KPPC AM Radio, Calif. - Disc Jockey

TEACHING EMPLOYMENT HISTORY: (Here you can include additional experience, not related to your objective)

Warren University, Warren, MI	08/1998 - present
Los Angeles University, Los Angeles, CA	07/2009 - present
Chef University, Charlestown, WV	10/2008 - present
Artesia University, Chicago, ILL	10/2008 - present

MEDIA AWARDS

- Alliance of Community Media Award - Best Local Newscast - Exec. Producer/News Dir./Anchor
- Cable Diamond Award - Best Community Event "Changing of the Guard: Police Chief Willie Williams" - Exec. Producer/Reporter
- Recognition Award for "Riot Coverage" - Greater Los Angeles Press Club - Exec. Prod./Reporter

PROFESSIONAL HONORS AND AFFILIATIONS:

*The National Political Science Honor Society *Delta Sigma Theta Sorority *Phi Sigma Alpha Honor Society *Sigma Delta Chi Professional Journalism Society *Outstanding Young Women of America

Also, some jobs require a Curriculum Vitae, which gives the employer a broader perspective of the potential employee and reveals other activities and skills that might be relevant to the qualifications of the available job position.

Include the following:

Curriculum Vitae:

- Objective
- Education - Institution, dates, concentration
- Management skills in detail - list companies, specific responsibilities, etc.
- Presentations, workshops, seminars, or trainings conducted
- Volunteer service
- Hobbies

There are several websites that provide a variety of formats. Google samples by using such key words as:

- Curriculum vitae.
- How to write a curriculum vitae for _____ (name your focus career), e.g., business, education, construction, CEO, etc.
- How to write a simple curriculum vitae.
- Tools for writing a curriculum vitae.
- Curriculum vitae builder.

CHAPTER 5

How a Solid Resume Opens Doors

How a Solid Resume Opens Doors

There is a difference between a "solid" resume and a "weak" one. Remember, the minute eyes are looking at your resume, the first look counts. If your resume looks unorganized, too long, out of order, too shallow, uninviting, or just plain unattractive, expect it to be passed up. The job hunting process begins with your personal introduction, which is your resume. Give it all you've got because that piece of paper represents not only your skills, but other talents such as being organized, creative, interesting, and simplistic, yet in control of your destiny. Don't take this lightly. Spend time with this "gem" to make it shine and sparkle; otherwise, expect for it to land in "the circular file". Skip colorful designs, unless the career expects more creativity than usual on a resume. Make sure your objective matches what the employer is seeking.

Remember, the resume is the key to your first formal interview. It is the door to an interview, and potentially a job. There are a variety of ways to write resumes, so it is essential that you research sample resumes for the specific job you are applying to before completing your own. It is not a case where "one size fits all". Make sure your job descriptions displayed on the resume match the qualifications that job seekers want. Use the same key words listed in the employer's description of a job in your resume. If the resume is submitted through the computer, those key words will match the job description and potentially lead you to the next step. Ask yourself, what am I bringing to the table?

If you are graduating from college and have little experience, matched terms will be key, even with minimal experience. For this reason, prior to graduating from college it is important to work, volunteer or intern at locations where job descriptions will match future job titles. Even if you have worked at establishments that do not match your future career goals, there will always be tasks that will be key to add to your resume. For example, if you worked at a fast-food place, and your goal is to work for a corporation in an office, be sure to mention the following that will help open the doors to an interview:

- Prompt.
- Met deadlines.
- Managed staff.
- Organizational skills.
- Public relations - people skills.
- Patience.
- Service-oriented.
- Key responsibilities - opened and closed - management trust - handled currency.
- Employee to employer relations.
- Ability to work in a team.
- Ability to work together.
- Leader and a follower.
- Ability to follow instructions.

These are just a few examples that will still be attractive to corporate America. However, keep in mind the job title and responsibilities that are needed to get the job. Be specific, and to the point, and deliver the message that even though you lack corporate experience, you still have the necessary skills to contribute to the company. Your message must be strong, solid, meaningful, and convincing. See your resume also as a persuasive argument. You need to persuade, lure, and convince the potential employee that the tools you are equipped with will be an asset, and the experience you may lack can be learned easily with a lot of hard work.

Depending on your job experience, you may want to consider one of the following types of resumes:

Chronological Resume: Experience current to the most recent employer is listed first.

Functional Resume: Reveals your work experience and strengths, as opposed to listing whom you have worked for in chronological order.

Hybrid Resume: This a combination of the chronological and functional resumes.

<u>Executive Resume:</u> This is for the applicant who has extensive professional work experience. This kind of resume targets each opportunity differently. Remember, every resume does not have to list everything one has done over the past 20 years for every job application. A corporation looking for an executive wants to know specifically what has this executive done that would benefit the company.

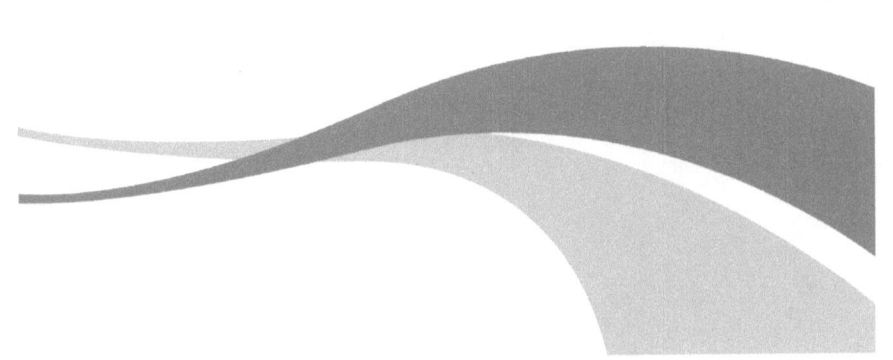

PART 2

THE INTERVIEW

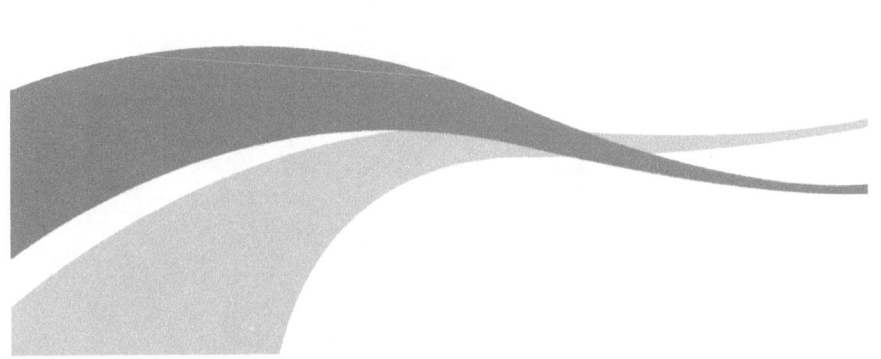

CHAPTER 6

"Dress to Impress" Still Applies to Today's Interviews

"Dress to Impress" Still Applies to Today's Interviews

Do you really know how to dress for a job interview? The first impression you make on a potential employer is the most important one because the interviewer's initial judgment is going to be based on how you look and what you are wearing. Research has shown that the first 100 seconds are crucial in determining the interviewer's perception of the candidate's suitability for the position. You never get a second chance to make a first impression. Research the industry that the job's a part of to familiarize yourself with the universal dress code. Ask a friend at the company or stop by the company in the morning hours before starting time to see what current employees wear on the job. How you should look varies depending on the type of industry and the job you are looking to secure. Take a look at general interview attire expectations for eight career areas:

- **Technology**

If you're applying for a technical position, you won't need a suit. Collared shirt and khakis or slacks would work. Same goes for women -- sweater or blouse and slacks or a skirt. But upgrade your attire if you're interviewing for a higher-level job and dress in the best clothes you have.

- **Finance**

Nothing is more precise and exact than managing money. You cannot afford to have a hair out of place. Full business, professional attire is required and expected.

- **Government**

At a government interview, don't be flashy. This is a time to show you're responsible, trustworthy, and honest. But a bit of color is OK, whether you're a man or a woman. The days of all white shirts for a man in government have ended. Be conservative with jewelry, makeup, and hairstyles.

- **Human Resources**

For a Human Resources interview, you must look professional and authoritative. You'll need to look like you can handle any crisis and be dependable.

- **Sales**

Typically, a suit is the uniform for a sales interview. After all, who would want to buy from a guy in a T-shirt and jeans? But you might be able to go with bolder designs and colors. The product or service you're representing will determine how classic versus trendy/fashionable you should be.

- **Automotive**

Here's an exception where a potential employer will understand if you have a little dirt or grease under your nails. You still want to look as neat as possible, but a suit is probably not necessary, unless you're interviewing at a high-end dealership. In that case, dress up a bit more.

- **Hospitality**

Image is particularly critical in the hospitality industry. A suit is appropriate for some positions, but not always a must. However, you always need to make a great initial impression.

- **Entertainment**

Depending on the genre will determine how to dress. Sometimes you might have to dress for a movie part or as extreme as a hip hop dancer. Know your industry.

- **Medical**

Dress professionally for medical positions, i.e., doctors, nurses, medical and dental assistants, and front office staff.

- **Trades**

Appropriate attire for an interview in the trades: Business casual. For men, this might be a nice pair of Dockers and a buttoned shirt along with well-kept and polished shoes. The same goes for women -- nice slacks and a professional, business top. A suit or sports jacket for this type of work is overkill. Of course, one industry's excess is another industry's underdressed.

So don't be afraid to ask because, no matter what, "your packaging counts". However, conservative is the safe option; most employers approve of suits. An interviewer is more likely to accept that you can dress down if the environment is more casual than that you will dress more conservatively once you are employed.

To avoid wearing the wrong outfit to an interview, always try on your clothes a few days before the appointment. Avoid doing this the day before because you might find out that a button is missing, the outfit is too tight or too short, or there's a stain on it, along with so many other mishaps that could happen to an outfit. The more you rush, the more nervous and unsettled you will be at an interview, so plan a few days ahead and determine what you will wear.

Tips and Warnings:

- No piercings.
- No chewing gum or candy.
- Cover up any tattoos as much as possible.
- Baggy clothes look messy and tight clothes look as though you are drawing attention to your looks rather than your skills!

- Jewelry, like ankle chains or toe rings, looks unprofessional and should be taken off for the interview.
- Keep it simple and smart

For Men:

Match the belt to the color of your shoes. Choose black if your outfit consists of dark grays, navys, browns, or blacks. Opt for dark brown if you'll be wearing tans, muted pastels, or medium-toned colors. Polish or clean your shoes the night before your interview. Scuff marks on your shoes reveal a lack of forethought and attention to detail.

Keep interview accessories professional. Take a briefcase or nice leather- or vinyl-bound portfolio to carry your resume references, or other pertinent documents. Leave tattered manila folders or college logo folders at home.

Avoid cologne or aftershave that may overpower the interviewer. Place your watch in your pocket once you make it to the front door so you're not tempted to look at it during the interview.

For Women:

One of the biggest self-killers of an interview is wearing clothes that do not fit you appropriately. That means that dresses too short or too tight, heels too high, too much make-up, shoes too casual, hair too wild, and so forth could end your job interview quicker than when you get started. Leave the oversized, disorganized handbag at home. It's better to dress too formally than to dress too casually. Trendy is fine, as long as you keep your style subtle. Clothes make a strong statement about you...What do you want to say?

Here's a quick look at the basics:

Men's Interview Attire

- Solid color, conservative suit
- White long-sleeved shirt
- Conservative tie

- Dark socks, professional shoes
- Very limited jewelry
- Neat, professional hairstyle
- Go easy on the aftershave
- Neatly trimmed nails
- Portfolio or briefcase

Women's Interview Attire

- Solid color, conservative suit
- Coordinated blouse
- Moderate shoes
- Limited jewelry
- Neat, professional hairstyle
- Tan or light hosiery
- Sparse make-up & perfume
- Manicured nails
- Portfolio or briefcase

What Not to Bring to the Interview

- Gum
- Cell phone
- iPod
- Coffee or soda
- If you have lots of piercings, leave some of your rings at home (earrings only is a good rule).
- Cover tattoos

Interview Attire Tips

- Before you even think about going on an interview, make sure you have appropriate interview attire and everything fits correctly.
- Get your clothes ready the night before, so you don't have to spend time getting them ready on the day of the interview.

- If your clothes are dry clean only, take them to the cleaners after an interview, so they are ready for next time.
- Polish your shoes.
- Eat a breath mint before you enter the building.

There's no getting around it: "In every job interview, you're going to be judged -- at least partially -- by how you look."

CHAPTER 7

Interview Tips to Get a Job

Interview Tips to Get a Job

Preparing for an interview is time-consuming and an involved process. Getting the interview may be seen as the greatest barrier to finding employment, but getting ready for an interview is another important step in finding the right job. Of course, not all interviews are equal. Some interviews may involve more pressure than others or require more preparation. For example, the interview for your first job after college could be the most nerve-racking of your career. Or the interview to get the big promotion you have always wanted could leave you sleepless for days. On the other hand, some interviews, like an interview for a job you are not sure you want, could seem unimportant. However you are feeling, there are certain steps that can be done to prepare. Even if the interview does not seem too important, always make a good impression.

• *Invest in Your Dress*

Always look your best at an interview. Women should wear their hair in a modern and appropriate style. For both men and women, hair should be recently washed and styled. Women should wear some makeup, but should never go over the top. Nails and hands should be moisturized and groomed. Clothes should be conservative, but also modern. Invest in a good suit! Taking the time to look great for an interview will not only impress the interviewer, it will give you a solid boost of confidence. People perform best when they look their best. Adhere to that famous adage: Dress for the job you want.

• *Know the Company*

It would be very embarrassing if the hiring manager asked you a question about the company and you either did not know or worse, got it wrong. Research everything you can about the company before the interview. Know it well enough to avoid verbal stumbles during the questions. Check to see if the company or its related industry has been in the news recently. Not only will this help you to prepare, you may get some insightful and well-thought out information from this research that will impress the interviewer.

• *Impress, Not Annoy*

The interview is a time to showcase your strengths and personality for the hiring manager. Your chances of employment will improve if you impress the interviewer, but there is a fine line between being impressive and being annoying. Answer questions in a way that focuses attention on strengths and abilities, but do not go on and on. No one wants to work with a braggart. When the interviewer asks if you have any questions, give a positive smile and proceed with a few prepared questions. Never walk into an interview with no idea of what you will ask at the end. An interviewer is looking for someone who can engage in conversation and wants to know more about the company and the position. It is always smart to ask about the day-to-day duties of the position or the reason the interviewer works for the company.

• *Demonstrate Enthusiasm*

No interviewer wants to spend time with someone who acts bored. When you arrive at the interview, initially say thank you for the opportunity to be there and how nice it is to meet the interviewer. Throughout the interview you should smile, pay attention, and acknowledge interest in the position. At the end, point out how your qualifications match the job description, so you would be a good candidate for the position. Thank the interviewer again. These verbal clues will help the interviewer to gauge your interest. Companies do not want to offer employment to someone who does not appear to desire the position.

• *Make Eye Contact*

Some people are naturally adept at making eye contact with others and engaging in conversation. If this skill does not come naturally to you, try to practice before an interview. It may seem odd to do so, but interviewers may be turned off by someone who cannot look them in the eye. Start with a mirror and try engaging yourself in conversation while maintaining eye contact. Ask a close friend or family member to work with you and hold eye contact during questions and answers.

• *Review Your Information*

Depending on the type of interview, you may be asked questions about what you know. For example, an interview for an engineering job may require answering questions about actual problems. Before you go to an interview, review basic facts related to your industry or desired career. You may want to look over old notes from college or from your previous employment and answer some example questions. You can never prepare too much.

Good luck with the interview process. Remember to always send a thank-you note after an interview and offer to contact the interviewer with any additional information. With the proper amount of preparation, the interview will be much more comfortable. Your employment opportunities are sure to increase with a great interview!

CHAPTER 8

The 25 Worst Job-Interviewing Mistakes

The 25 Worst Job-Interviewing Mistakes

For fun, emotional security, and the thrill of anticipation, the job interview ranks right up there with IRS audits, going on your first roller-coaster ride, or going for your first bungee jump! And if being judged makes you nervous, you're in for a great ride! In the current job market with hundreds of qualified job applicants all vying for that one great opening, it's like going for an open casting call in the next Steven Spielberg movie. Getting an audition just means surviving until the last round.

A major part of the job interview is avoiding the unmistakable wrongs. Avoid making the following 25 mistakes, and you're apt to land the job.

1. ARRIVING LATE

Nothing makes a worse impression. If you can't even show up on time for the interview, how on earth would you do as an employee? If there's even a remote chance that weather, traffic, unfamiliar locations, poor directions, or car trouble might be a problem, leave early just to be sure. If you are not certain about the location or parking, drive to the site the day before to avoid any problems.

2. ARRIVING EARLY

Arriving at the interview location at 9:30 for a 10:00 o'clock appointment is good – checking in with the receptionist is not. You don't want to put pressure on your interviewer, nor do you want to pace in the lobby and wear a path into the marble floor! Instead, go to a nearby restaurant for a coffee. Then return to your interview 10 minutes prior to your appointment.

3. DRESSING INCORRECTLY

First impressions are important. Cleanliness and neatness in grooming and attire project a confident attitude. Frequently, the decision is made in the first few minutes of the interview whether it's going to be a turn down, a second interview, or a hire. The first impression will dictate the length of your interview and your opportunity to present yourself. As a general rule, corporate business attire is a suit and tie for men and tailored suit or dress for women in a conservative color such as black, navy, gray, or tan with appropriate footwear. No tennis shoes for men and closed-toed shoes for women with a low heel and hose. Avoid any extremes in hair style (including color), make-up, perfumes, colognes, and jewelry. Keep it simple.

4. DRESSING IN A HURRY

Don't do it. If you choose your clothes 10 minutes before you have to leave for your interview, you'll wind up with mismatched socks or those shoes with the loose heel or that shirt with the missing button. Pick your interviewing outfit a day or two before, try it on, and have it set out the evening before your interview.

5. NOT DOING ALL OF YOUR HOMEWORK BEFORE THE INTERVIEW

It isn't necessary to memorize the company's annual sales and projects, but you should know something about their products and services. You can learn about most companies on the Internet, in business magazines, or in the library, or you can call the company and ask for a copy of their annual report.

6. SMOKING

Studies show that executives and hiring authorities surveyed would hire a non-smoker over a smoker, if their qualifications were equal. Most office buildings and common areas are now regulated by city codes that disallow smoking. If you smoke on the drive to your interview, your clothes will smell of smoke, and it will be noticeable to most individuals when you come in contact within a non-smoking environment. Even if it's allowed, smoking during the interview generally gives an impression of nervousness.

7. DRINKING

As some interviews are conducted during lunch, dinner, networking events, or other similar environments, your interviewer or others may be ordering cocktails. Even though others are indulging, you are better off sticking with mineral water or club soda. At the very most, order a white wine spritzer and stick to one. You want to be alert and at your best, not mellowed out.

8. CHEWING GUM

Have you ever asked for help at a mini-mart and the sales clerk is chomping away on gum? Have you ever wanted to take that sales person behind the counter and make him spit it out? Take this example and don't do it. No gum at all during an interview.

9. BRINGING ALONG A FRIEND OR A RELATIVE

Enticing as it may be to have someone along to hold your hand or help you fill out an application, it could cost you the job. Being dropped off, picked up, or even being seen saying goodbye to your friend, parent, or spouse at the building door can make you look as if you don't have the nerve to go out on your own. You also don't want the interviewer to think you must depend on someone else to get to work.

10. SKIPPING A DRESS REHEARSAL

You wouldn't make a speech or talk in front of your PTA or church group without planning what you were going to say, yet people walk into their job interviews every day assuming they will be able to answer any questions off the top of their heads. Don't assume! Make a list of the questions you would ask if you were interviewing someone else for this job, and then rehearse the best possible answers. If you have already been on an interview, go over the questions you felt you could have answered better. Use a tape recorder, listen to yourself, and do some role-playing with a friend or relative.

11. ADMITTING A FLAW

Inevitably, you will be asked by the interviewer, "What is your greatest weakness?" or "If you need improvement, in what area would it be?" Giving a straightforward, totally honest answer is a mistake the interviewer doesn't expect you to make. It's all part of the interviewer's technique to have you eliminate yourself from the competition. Answer the question with a positive weakness such as, "I'm a very organized person, but you'd never know it from looking at my desk."

12. NOT KNOWING YOUR OWN STRENGTHS

You must know your background and your resume thoroughly so you are prepared to answer any question without hesitation. If you are asked a question about your background, such as dates, you shouldn't have to refer to your resume. Hesitating, being vague, or groping for the right words destroys the impression you are trying to create. Make a list of ten work-related items you do well or know about. Then, during your interview, come up with graceful ways to bring them up.

13. ASKING TOO MANY QUESTIONS

If you were the interviewer, would you hire someone who took over the conversation, hijacked the entire interview, and put you on the defensive? Keep your questions relevant to the position and be brief.

14. NOT ASKING ANY QUESTIONS

On the other hand, when the interviewer asks, "Do you have any questions?" It is a bad idea not to have any questions. You may look uninterested, unimaginative, or like you didn't pay attention during the interview, or all three. If you can't think of any questions, rely on the homework you have done. Let's say you are interviewing for a position in the real estate market. Having done your research on the strength of the market, you may ask, "Do you expect the market in this area to remain as strong as it has been in the past six months?"

15. INQUIRING ABOUT BENEFITS TOO SOON

Ask not what the company can do for you, but what you can do for the company!

Sound familiar? If you seem more interested in the profit-sharing plan and vacation policy than the job duties and requirements, the prospective employer will develop serious concerns about your priorities. Of course, you have the right to know about the benefits a company offers, but chances are the company information will be offered. After all, their benefits are a selling point. If the subject isn't brought up, you can broach the subject when salary negotiations begin. Explain the offer you'll accept depends on the value of the whole compensation package.

16. REVEALING YOUR PRICE TAG

Did you ever go window-shopping and fall in love with an item you had to have before checking to see how much it cost? It may have taught you to look at the price right away so you can reject the item mentally before having your heart set on it. Interviewing for a job is pretty similar. Let your interviewers discover how wonderful you are before you tell them how much you cost. If they try to sneak a premature peak at your price tag, let them know you have given the salary some thought but you need to know more about what the job entails. In many instances, you will already know the company's salary range and they will assume you fall into their criterion if you are interviewing.

17. CRYING DISCRIMINATION

There are guidelines and laws about questions which can and cannot be asked during the interview. The problem is not everyone involved in the hiring process knows which questions are not allowed - and in complete innocence, the interviewer may bring up a prohibited question. If your prospective employer asks you how you manage to work full-time and take care of your children, he may be genuinely interested or just making conversation to set you both at ease. Don't jump up and scream accusations. Instead, reassure your interviewer that you can handle all of your responsibilities. Even if the employer's intentions are not honorable, a dramatic protest is unlikely to get you the job offer. If you don't get hired due to the responses of inappropriate questioning, you can file a complaint. If you do get hired, you can bring up the issue later as a full-fledged employee and make important changes for the company's benefit from the inside.

18. BAD-MOUTHING YOUR PREVIOUS EMPLOYER

Don't ever, ever say anything derogatory or negative about an employer, coworker, or company you have worked for in the past. It marks you as a complainer. It's a small world and you don't know the person who's interviewing you and whom the interviewer knows.

19. THE NAME GAME

Don't drop names. Attempts to play "who do you know" games with your interviewer may have an unfortunate tendency to backfire on you. Drop the name of someone at the company and it could turn out to be the hiring manager's worst enemy! Announce that you went to school with the chairman of the board's daughter, Mary, and it may come off as elitism. Even worse, the interviewer may wonder why Mary didn't ask her father to put in a good word for you. A much better approach is to use inside contacts. Ask them to recommend or introduce you to the powers that be.

20. LACK OF ENERGY

It doesn't matter if you only slept four hours last night and are coming down with a cold, when you get to the interviewer you have to appear bright-eyed and eager. You must be cordial and polite. Job candidates with a lackluster demeanor or an attitude rarely get the job offer. Mental energy is what it takes, so psych yourself up before making your entrance. Some lecturers and TV talk show hosts do it by playing lively music right before going on. If that's impossible, just play an upbeat tune in your head. Think of yourself as an entertainer and know that the show must go on!

21. HANDSHAKE FAILURE

A limp or otherwise distasteful handshake is like bad breath, one of those things even your best friends may never tell you about. Test out your handshake. Try this. Go to a trusted friend or relative and ask, "If I were going to develop the world's most perfect handshake, would I make mine a little firmer, a little shorter, softer, longer, or what?" Then shake your friend's hand to demonstrate. Even if the interviewer does not offer a handshake, offer yours.

22. GLANCING AT YOUR WATCH

Clock-watching gives the impression you are late for a more important date, bored, or uninterested. Avoid this problem by asking when you set up the appointment how much time you should allow for the entire interview. Your interviewer may be running behind, you may have to complete an application or take some tests, or you may be asked to meet with another decision-maker.

23. PLAYING THE SUPERSTAR

In 999 jobs out of 1,000, you're going to be called to work as part of the team, not to make a single-handed rescue of a botched effort. Never convey the message "you guys really have a problem here, but I can show you how to turn this company around." Instead, express how well your talents and experience mesh with those of others in the department, division, or company.

24. LOSING YOUR COOL

Expect the unexpected. Occasionally, interviewers have been known to test job applicants by surprising them with loaded questions or blunt comments such as, "What makes you think you can handle this job when people with twice your experience don't try to apply?" Remain calm even though your injured ego may be fleeing for the nearest exit. Some interviewers like to see just how professional you remain and how spontaneous.

25. FOLLOWING INSTRUCTIONS

You may be given an application to complete or test to take. Make sure you complete the entire application even if you have a resume. There may be questions on the application that are not addressed in your resume. Never give an answer on an application "see resume." Leaving questions blank, unanswered, or referring to your resume shows your inability to take direction, impatience levels, and your unwillingness to follow follow instructions.

Finally, there is an art to interviewing, so it may take a few interviews to get the hang of it. Use your interviews and your mistakes as learning tools to improve on future interviews.

Now you know the do's and don'ts of interviewing, so go out and get that job!

CHAPTER 9

Bring a Positive Mindset to Your Next Interview

Bring a Positive Mindset to Your Next Interview

Landing the important first job after college can be a source of sleepless nights. There's so much advice out there about what to wear, what to say, and what to do that it's hard to know where to start. So, rather than going through a lengthy list of do's and don'ts, you have to focus on building a positive mindset.

Let's say you know what type of job you want. You've researched companies, come up with a winning resume, and have enough "dress for success" fashions in your closet. You're ready to go out and get that job. There's just one other task you need to do: ace the interview. This is usually where things fall apart.

It seems easy enough. Just make an appointment. Show up on time and put your best foot forward, right? Well, yes and no. You do have to make a good impression, but most people go overboard. In their enthusiasm—or desperation—they forget about what they really want or need in their desire to please the interviewer. Desperation makes people uneasy and many job seekers are unaware that they are sending out these negative vibes. Employers subconsciously pick up on the messages and reject these applicants. It is important not to approach job hunting from the standpoint of need even if you're down to your last package of Top Ramen. What ends up happening is that no one is pleased, especially the interviewer. People can sense insincerity or a lack of confidence, regardless of that $400 suit you may be wearing.

So, how do you ace the interview and be yourself? Is it really possible? Here's what you need to remember:

- The person on the other side of the desk is a human being, complete with personal flaws and insecurities. The interviewer may be as uneasy talking to a total stranger as you are.
- Don't just sit there answering question after question. Show interest in the position by firing off a few questions of your own.
- Value your time. If you're hired, you will give up 40 or more hours of your life each week for an indefinite amount of time. Of course, you need the money, but you can get that from a number of possible jobs. Your time (your life) can't be replaced by anyone.
- Carefully study your resume and memorize a few key points. Be prepared to explain anything it covers as well as items it does not. If your work history is spotty - not uncommon during an economic crisis - anticipate what you may be asked in order to prepare a positive response.

Here are a few examples of how to respond:

1. Question: Why do you want to work for ABC Company?

   Answer: "My research shows ABC is a growing company..."

2. Question: Why should we hire you?

   Answer: "I believe I meet all (or most) of the important qualifications. I have 'X' number of years in the industry..."

   If you really feel confident, answer the same question this way: "You should hire me because you like me!" A friend of mine gave this unexpected response and was hired on the spot. It's a fact that, all things being equal, employers will hire those whom they like the most. It's a natural human reaction.

Never speak badly about a former employer. While the interviewer may listen with interest or even sympathize, badmouthing your boss is unattractive. No one wants to be around whiners and complainers, especially when you haven't been hired yet.

Sometimes job seekers ruin their own chances because they feel bad about themselves. They may feel responsible for being fired or let go from their last job. A new job means a new start. So, do some soul searching. Ask yourself what you will do differently in your next job to make yourself more valuable. Decide that your career is too important to hold grudges—even with yourself.

Here's a quote to remember from the late author Eric Butterworth: "As you sit thinking, 'If only I could find a job,' some employer is at that very moment thinking, 'If only we could find the right person to fill this position.'"

You are not some needy person trying to make something of yourself against all odds. You are a valuable person with a dream to fulfill and a purpose to express. As you gather your resume and put on your Sunday best, you must put on a winning attitude. Then, you'll really be dressed for success.

CHAPTER *10*

20 Ways to Make a Great First Impression

20 Ways to Make a Great First Impression

So, you're a graduating senior and you have a job interview a week from today. With the job market as tight as it is – and no relief in sight – it is imperative you do everything you can, not only to make a good first impression, but also to make the person with whom you're interviewing want to hire you. After all, while chances are good you're a sharp cookie with a stellar academic record, that's probably also the case for the other five people vying for the position. Given that, here are a few tips you may want to consider before your job interview.

1. Arrive at least 15 minutes early for your interview.

This will show the prospective employer you fully understand the importance of being on time – and flexibility. After all, if you're 15 minutes early and the interviewer has had an unexpected scheduling change, starting your interview early may help him or her. Also, if you're supposed to report to work at 8 a.m., which means at 8 a.m., you're already in the building, at your computer or work station, and working. It does NOT mean at 8 a.m. you're walking hurriedly through the door or, even worse, pulling into a parking space.

2. Dress appropriately.

The way you dress says a lot about you, and it can be a red flag to a prospective employer. If you don't dress appropriately for a job interview – suit and tie for men, nice suit or dress for women – it tells a prospective employer you likely won't dress appropriately at work or when you're away representing them on company business.

3. Sit patiently in the waiting area until you're called for the interview.

In other words, don't talk loudly or excessively on the telephone while you're waiting. The administrative assistant who's going to walk you back to the prospective employer's office for the interview will likely be "listening in" on your conversation and could later reveal to the interviewer some or all of what was heard. Likewise, don't gesture or act impatient if you have to wait beyond the scheduled interview time. Your interview may be at 11 a.m., but the person interviewing you could get tied up until 11:15 a.m. Wait patiently. For all you know, it could be a test simply to see whether you have patience.

4. Be polite to the administrative assistant.

Make it a point to greet her or him by name – if a nameplate is visible – or at least by saying ma'am or sir. You'd be surprised how many bosses seek input from administrative assistants when deciding whom to make an offer to for a job. Also, be sure to thank the administrative assistant both after he/she leads you into the office for the interview and as you're leaving the building.

5. Accept bottled water if offered.

You may be offered coffee or juice if it's a morning interview, but with coffee you'll have the distraction of adding cream and sugar, and water shows you're health-conscious. Even if you're really not thirsty, it's probably a good idea to accept some water.

6. Look the interviewer directly in the eye and give a firm – but not too hard – handshake.

Not looking the prospective employer in the eye may signal, unjustly, that you're shy or meek. And no one likes limp handshakes.

7. Don't answer questions too quickly.

Certainly wait until the prospective employer has gotten the question completely out of his or her mouth before you begin answering.

8. Don't take too long to answer questions.

Taking too long may imply you're struggling to come up with an answer. Employers like employees who are quick on their feet.

9. Don't let your answers go on endlessly.

While it's good to give thoughtful answers, you don't want to go on and on and on and put the interviewer to sleep. Give good, concise answers and keep it moving!

10. Don't appear too cocky.

You know you're highly qualified for the job, but let the answers to your questions – and your resume – prove it to the employer. Don't come across as a cocky, know-it-all because it can spell doom for you.

11. Do your homework on the company at which you're applying.

Nothing is more embarrassing than when a person shows up ill-prepared for a job interview. The prospective employer isn't going to expect you to know as much about the company as he/she, but you must take time before the interview – not while you're waiting in the lobby to be called back – to learn about the company. If the person with whom you're interviewing is the "head honcho," certainly take time to do your research on him or her.

12. Be complimentary of the interviewer without sucking up.

Take a second or two to glance around the interviewer's office. If he/she has degrees or awards displayed on the wall, perhaps you could mention it during one of your answers. Or, you might want to compliment his tie or her shoes. But, please ensure your compliment sounds sincere and not like you're trying to suck up. If you cannot compliment the interviewer without sounding disingenuous, it's probably best you skip the compliment altogether.

13. Put your best foot forward.

Some people call it sending a representative. In other words, make sure you give it your best shot during the interview. After all, you may not get another chance to impress the person with whom you're interviewing. Don't leave the interview and then think of better ways you should have answered questions, because by then it's too late.

14. Get a good night's sleep before your interview.

There are not many things worse than showing up for an interview looking tired and disheveled. And I guarantee you, constant yawning during an interview won't bode well for your chances of getting the offer. Get a good night's sleep the night before your interview. It will do you wonders!

15. Be honest about your proficiencies.

If you are not proficient in one or two of the 20+ duties listed in the job description, be honest about it. A prospective employer will respect you for being honest about a deficiency, but will dislike it if you lie about your skill level – only to have the truth reveal itself once you've been hired.

16. Know what to disclose.

If your mother, father, brother, sister, or spouse used to work at the company, you should reveal it in the interview. However, if your fifth cousin twice removed used to work there, that's probably not worth mentioning. Of course, if your mother, father, brother, sister, or spouse was justifiably fired, you should decide before the interview whether that's a place at which you should be applying in the first place.

17. Don't let Facebook do you in.

We live in a technology age. Employers routinely examine the Facebook pages of prospective employees, so be sure you don't have anything on your Facebook page that could bite you in the "you-know-what" during an interview.

18. Don't make off-color jokes or remarks during your interview.

We also live in an age of political correctness. Don't say anything during your interview that could be deemed offensive. Don't make jokes about sexuality, race, gender, or religion. If the prospective employer makes jokes about sexuality, race, gender, or religion – don't laugh. Also, don't get "too comfortable" during your interview. The prospective employer could have Black Power posters all over his or her wall, but you still need not say anything negative about Caucasians or any other race of people. For all you know, his or her spouse could be white. Staying away from politics is also advisable during interviews.

19. Make sure your resume is up-to-date, factual, and impressive.

Don't have grammatical errors and/or typos on your resume. Make sure your resume is impressive, but also ensure it's not over the top or too busy.

20. Follow up with a thank-you card.

This may sound old-fashioned, particularly given the technology age in which we live, but employers still appreciate getting thank-you cards in the mail. Do not do anything fancy. Just write a brief note to thank the interviewer for the opportunity to be interviewed for the position. You never know what's going to give you the edge over another candidate; however, be sure you have the person's correct name and title, and spell them correctly, before sending a card.

CHAPTER *11*

Salary Negotiations
– Be Prepared

Salary Negotiations – Be Prepared

Negotiating a salary is probably one of the most difficult parts of a job interview. It could also be one of your worst moments if you are not satisfied after accepting the offer. It's not always easy to talk about the salary at an interview, even though the employer knows that you are eager to get to that point. Somehow asking about the salary has become a major taboo, as though you want the salary, not necessarily the job that comes along with it. But let's face it, salaries attract job seekers, even if the job doesn't become a long-term career. Sometimes you just want to get into the door of a company and make a good salary to start.

A mistake job seekers, who become very desperate for employment, end up making is asking for a salary that is just too low. Big mistake, especially when you find out, after accepting the position, that the last person was making much more. Ouch!!! That really hurts and you begin to regret accepting the job, and even promising to do all of the tasks that come along with the job. On the other side of the coin, the regret can also be asking for a salary that is too high and you've just excluded yourself from a potential hire.

To prepare for that big question, "What kind of salary are you looking for?", do your homework and be smart about it before negotiating with a company. Be prepared and don't talk about a salary too soon. Let them ask the question. However, keep in mind that the employer will usually negotiate down and never up the salary chart. Here are other tips on getting the salary you deserve:

*Research the job title and match it up with your experience to see what salaries are being paid at other companies. Use these companies as an example when negotiating salary and experience.

*If there is a salary range, and you have very "limited" experience, avoid taking the top salary; instead, work with the employer and go mid-way, but never to the bottom. If you are right out of college, throw in your other skills, such as good character, well-organized, prompt, deadline-oriented and so forth. Just because a person has experience does not mean that they have all of the other skills that a company desires in a candidate.

*If you want the highest salary on the chart, point out your expertise, quality of work, dedication, and longevity with past employers.

*Never settle or avoid negotiating, which gives the power to the employer. Always have a bottom-line figure in mind before walking into salary negotiations. Never try to make that decision on the spot. If they make you an offer, and you have not thought about it, tell them you will consider the package they are offering and let them know by the end of the day or the next day what would work for both of you.

*Never let them know your bottom line of what you will accept. Let them know that you will consider a figure, after you look at the entire package deal you are being offered.

*Don't compare your former lower salary with the new job offer. Employers like to compare your past salaries, especially if they were much lower than their salary scale, by pointing out that their lowest salary is much more than if you stayed at your previous job. Your past salaries have nothing to do with new negotiations. When leaving a job, most people want to make a higher salary, substantially, so your past salary should not be a guideline point for you or the employer. Base your salary request on your new tasks and experiences, and what you have to offer to the company.

*When negotiating, you should have already made a list of what it takes for you to survive and to live comfortably. Figure out your lowest salary that will give you the comfort you deserve for working 40 plus hours per week.

*If the employer offers you a salary and you really do not like it, wait at least 24 to 48 hours before declining or accepting it. Your first thought would be to decline it because you can't believe they are offering something so low. However, factor in the company benefits, healthcare plans, and convenience before turning this opportunity down. If you are not satisfied with the lower salary, ask how often raises are given. It might not be long before you actually are making the salary you desire.

*Don't negotiate a salary to death. Employers don't have time to go back and forth too many times, unless it is a high-powered executive position where negotiations could take days and even weeks. Be reasonable, but stick to your guns. You must determine, however, how badly you want the job and is negotiating a salary back and forth and risking the employer's decline worth it? Decide this before negotiations begin.

The bottom line is whatever you end up accepting, live with it and with no regrets. Do the best you can to move up the ladder, and equally important, be even smarter at negotiating a salary at the next job interview.

CHAPTER *12*

Is It the Interview Or Just Me? Can't Find Employment Or A New Career?

Is it the Interview or Just Me?

CAN'T FIND EMPLOYMENT OR A NEW CAREER?

It is now time to look for a job or change careers, but no luck yet. You might be tired of the same process of looking for a job or even tired of being rejected. No matter what the case, you might be blocking your own chance to succeed, simply because your qualifications may not have changed.

Along with the normal process of finding a new job or changing careers, seriously think about upgrading your skills. Just because you are already employed, educated, or highly skilled, employment is not just around the corner. And if it is, the salary might be the same. Why? Because you are the same. With no new skills, no new certifications, and no upgrade of your education, why should anything be different?

Don't fret, you are not alone. However, to solve this problem, if you want a change in your life, especially financially, and a new career, prepare for it ahead of time. Don't just wake up one day and look for a job. Have a strategic plan to land employment. This plan is set in advance before searching for a job. If you know that the job you have is not your career choice or you want to make more money, or you just need to find employment, ask yourself the following questions:

- **What career would be fulfilling long-term?**
  - *Think hard and long so that you don't keep changing careers.*

- **What skills are needed to find a desired career?**
  - *List them one by one. This is where researching plays a major role with your preparation for finding the most desirable job.*

- **What do I need to accomplish to obtain those skills?**
  - *Seek ways to improve and expand your skills. What does the job require and what do you lack?*

- **How do I know how to enhance my skills?**
  - *Always research what the career entails and what you can do extra to stand out from the hundreds who are also looking for*

the same job. *This might mean going back to school, taking a few certification programs, or receiving more training. This can be done through accelerated college programs, adult schools, online companies, and through your current employer.*

How can I become more focused on what I want to do?

- *Along with researching for the type of career you want and the skills you need to land a job, you can also specifically focus on individual companies where you could spend the next decade or more working. Those under 50 could switch to another company when an opportunity arises, if necessary. However, the more matured adult, in age, who is getting ready for retirement, should focus on researching a company based on retirement benefits as well as career goals, and plan to stay there until the time of retirement.*

- **When do I want this to occur in my life?**
  - *Put together a realistic timetable that is detailed of what needs to be accomplished to get the job. Some might believe that a monthly plan should be sufficient; however, creating a daily or weekly schedule could keep your momentum going in order to achieve your goals sooner than later. Equally important is to avoid making the timetable too far out so that you don't lose confidence or momentum, or simply give up.*

- **What to do with my timetable?**
  - *Follow it day after day, tirelessly. Take action. Make it happen.*

So, when all is said and done, do more than just the process of finding a job, but be prepared before you begin the search. These tips are simple, yet effective, in an effort to assist with changing your unemployment status to employed, and creating a plan that will push your career in the right direction and make your work days more profitable and rewarding. Taking the first step is the hardest, but once you get started, and see results, there will be no stopping you from succeeding. Stay confident, diligent, and positive.

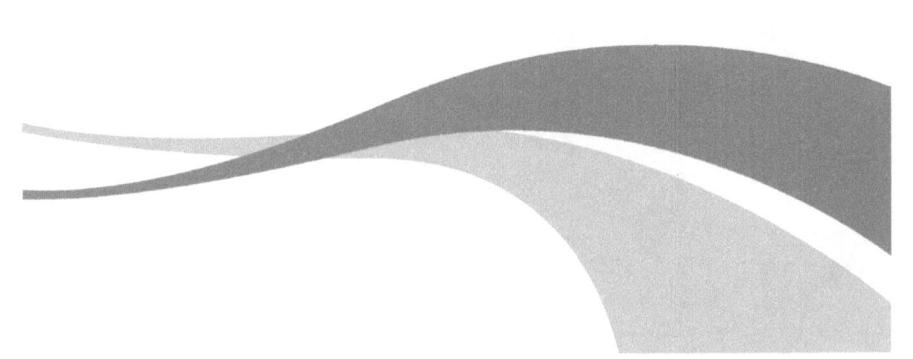

PART 3

EXITING THE INTERVIEW

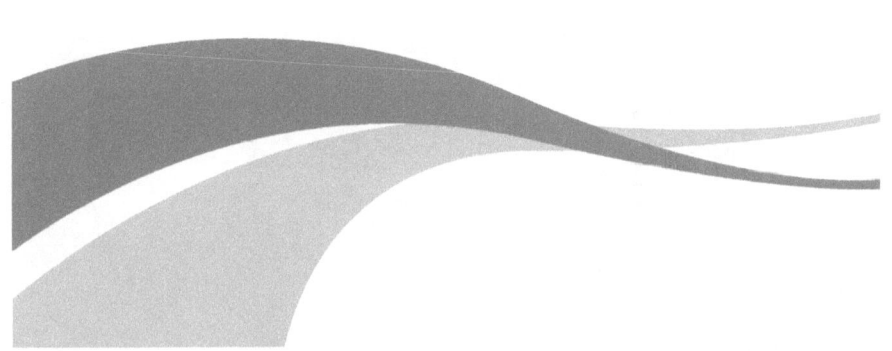

CHAPTER 13

Following Up Without Being Annoying

Following Up Without Being Annoying

Can't wait to know if you've got the job or an interview? Well, this is when you need to put on your patience hat and give the company time to digest information from your application that was followed by probably hundreds more. If you followed the guidelines, especially the ones in this book, don't worry. While you are waiting for a call from one employer, continue to look for other career possibilities. You know the old saying, "Don't put all of your eggs in one basket." Keep looking and exploring opportunities.

You could end up with several interviews, which allows you to pick the company to work for and not be desperate to take whatever is offered to you.

Follow up with a thank-you letter; even if it doesn't get read, your name will be highlighted again. Remember that employers may be secretly looking to replace someone they have not dismissed yet or maybe they want to see what is available if they expand their department. There are several reasons employers open up job positions. Some may be actively hiring and some may not.

If you do not hear from a company in a month or two, dropping them an email or note is appropriate. Let them know you are still interested. Never assume that because months have passed that the employer has rejected your application. If you do not receive a notice of rejection, don't assume. Stay positive and keep looking. Keep an eye on the company in the news and on job sites to see the activity of the company.

There is so much you can be doing while waiting for a response after submitting your application to a company. Look through social media sites, particularly where professionals post information, and see if you find anyone who works for the company you are applying or have applied to, in order to make a connection that might lead to a job. Make a connection with them. That person could be your direct link to the person hiring. This will help to get your mind off of making too many calls to the human resources department or directly to the person filling the job position.

Overall, keep yourself busy. Wait patiently. Don't give up hope. Continue to look for employment. Keep an eye on the company's employment section and activity. Try to meet someone from the company on social media. Continue to enhance your skills.

CHAPTER 14

Closing the Interview

Closing the Interview

Just as the sweaty palms have started to cool, the butterflies in the tummy have flown away, and the nervousness in your throat has calmed, it all returns right before you give the final handshake and say your goodbyes to the person who holds the key to your future. Everything you felt at the beginning of the interview returns. Why does this happen? Because you do not know what to say at the closing of the interview! Therefore, you are not confident you landed the job.

Echoed at 98 percent of interviews, the famous final words – "Well, is there anything you'd like to add?" The answer should never be NO! You should always have something to say at the end of an interview. If you do not, then your interviewer thinks you did not listen to anything that was said. Why? Because most interviews have a built-in follow-up question, usually several, that you, as the interviewee, are expected to ask somewhere within the interview. Nodding your head and showing off that big pretty smile are not enough signals to get the job, even if you are qualified.

Employers want to know you are a good listener, curious, and a critical thinker. Remember, these follow-up questions are built in and need some sort of response from the interviewee.

What to Do?

Be prepared. Have a list of questions to learn more about the company that, of course, could not be answered on their website or in literature, which you should have already read.

Another strategy is to ask questions about how the job was handled by the last employee. What was most significant to the company? What needs to be changed or done that would greatly benefit the company?

If the conversation gets relaxed and has turned to personal interests and you have something in common, make it known. However, do not get too relaxed and avoid diving too deeply into the interviewer's personal life.

To get prepared with follow-up questions, take notes as the

interviewer is talking. They like to see you are taking an interest and making note of important elements about the job. Do not, however, enter into an interview and ask for a pen or a piece of paper. You might as well turn around and go to the closest burger joint and indulge in your sad food, because you would have lost the job before you uttered your first words.

Moving right along, be ready to ask follow-up questions when appropriate. You do not have to wait until the end of the interview. You should ask the follow-up question while on the topic. However, if you cannot appropriately interject your own thoughts into the conversation, wait patiently, listen well, and then when the interviewer asks the famous question, say, "Yes, I have a few follow-up questions."

Warning:

Warning I: Be sure to make it known you have follow-up questions. Try not to wait until the interviewer says, "Well, if you don't have anything else, that should be all for today. Thanks for coming." It is too late if you wait until the "Thanks for coming" line.

Warning II: Do not conduct your own interview. Avoid keeping the interviewer there another hour. Remember you are just making sure the employer knows you were paying attention and listening. You want the employer to know you are intuitive, inquisitive, and a good listener.

Concern:

Now, if you had the chance to ask follow-up questions throughout the interview and the interviewer has basically answered all of the questions you had, what do you do? This is where your skills of being all that you can be, responding on your feet, and being a quick thinker come into play.

Walk into the interview with questions. Mark them off as they are answered. You can ask the questions that were not addressed. However, if all have been addressed, then you must think of questions to ask while you are still listening to the interviewer, so you do not ask a question that has already been asked or have nothing to say at the end of the interview.

The closing question does not have to be complex in any way. However, it must have meaning, relevance, and quality to it. For example, if I were to start the job next week, what would be the company's first goal they'd want me to achieve?

Your job is to convince the interviewer you're right for the job. Leave with a good impression.

Closing the Interview Review Tips:

Take notes.

Never say, "No, I do not have any more questions. You have basically covered it all."

Avoid getting too relaxed and personal. "Too" being the key word here.

Do not have more than two to three short follow-up questions at the end of the interview when the interviewer asks the famous question.

If you have three questions, for example, avoid asking them back-to-back. Ask a question, wait for an answer. Ask a question, wait for an answer.

Make your follow-up questions short and to the point.

Ask your questions at the end only if you did not have an opportunity to ask them within the interview.

Even if you had a chance to ask follow-up questions within the interview, you must still have at least one or two questions before the famous closing line – "Thanks for coming."

Avoid appearing as though you are taking control of the interview – SIDE NOTE - You always want to be in control, but do not appear to be taking over – there is a difference. Ask your question, listen for the response, and then move on.

The closing of the interview is as important as the first impression. You want to close strongly. Asking the right questions will validate the strength of your resume. Also, before leaving the interview, make sure the employer knows you are still interested in the position and you can take it to the success level that is desired by the company.

CHAPTER 15

Leaving Your Job? Exit Gracefully and Don't Burn Bridges

Leaving Your Job? Exit Gracefully and Don't Burn Bridges

While much time justifiably is spent in preparation for your introductory job interview, far too little time is spent on the other end of the spectrum - the exit interview. Perhaps it's understandable, when you consider they're not always mandatory and often seen as a last step before you hand in your ID badge and set sail to your next professional endeavor. You may have the desire to use the process as an opportunity to offer the former employer helpful advice for improving the workplace ... or worse ... making the mistake of thinking it's an opportunity to air out long-held grievances, but do neither. While the impulse to tell off your old boss, former colleagues, or anyone else who might have crossed you in some manner may be overwhelming, it's best to hold your tongue and find a more civil, restrained manner of explaining the reason you're choosing to leave the company. "No one wants to hear your dirty laundry, so save it for the dry cleaners," said Gail Yoshimoto Shih, director of employment for Knight Ridder, No. 28 on The DiversityInc Top 50 Companies for Diversity list.

Sometimes, employees misconstrue the exit interview as their opportunity to go after the manager or co-worker they didn't get along with. But you need to be careful not to tell tales which are inappropriate or beyond the scope of the interview. This is not the time to shine the light on the evils of a co-worker or the manager you didn't like. Whenever you speak negatively about a person or situation you were involved in, you run the risk of appearing like a sour grape who may have a problem working with others. It's important to leave with grace. The types of questions you should expect could be: "Why are you leaving?", "What did you enjoy or dislike about working here?" or "How did you get along with your supervisor?" From a management perspective, the exit interview provides the company with an opportunity to learn the reason an employee is leaving the organization and determine if there are any systemic issues which led to the departure. While rarely mandatory, exit interviews are requested of most employees, as they give the organization an opportunity to ensure a fellow employee won't be leaving the organization six months later for the same reason. You want to focus as much as possible on what you enjoyed about the experience. Even if you had constant disagreements with your former boss, reflect on the experience in the most positive terms. Express enthusiasm for the projects where you excelled, and thank the employer for the time to work and grow at the company. You can always find something positive to say. Please don't use the exit interview to knock someone down - that's not its purpose.

If for no other reason than self-preservation, there are reasons to be cautious. For one, while it may seem unlikely at the time, you actually may decide you'd like to rejoin the company in the future, so you don't want to leave under a dark cloud. Secondly, even if you don't return to the firm, you never know where that former boss or colleague you've just thrown under a bus could turn up. "That old supervisor could end up at another company somewhere down the line and your paths could cross again," warned Shih. "It's always a very small community." Another aspect to keep in mind is the all-important job reference. If you leave the organization in an unprofessional manner, the chance of obtaining a useful reference from the employer down the line is almost nonexistent. Also, keep in mind that people talk or insinuate. Even if the human resources director is legally bound to only provide basic information about you to potential future employers, non-verbal or subtle hints about how you left the company could come back to haunt you.

Shih noted, "The exit interviewer might also go into specifics about relationships with their managers. We'll also ask them where they are going. You have to understand that as an employee, the exit interview is the last impression you are leaving, and it's the one that will be remembered. So, it's important to leave the workplace the same way you came in…with grace and dignity."

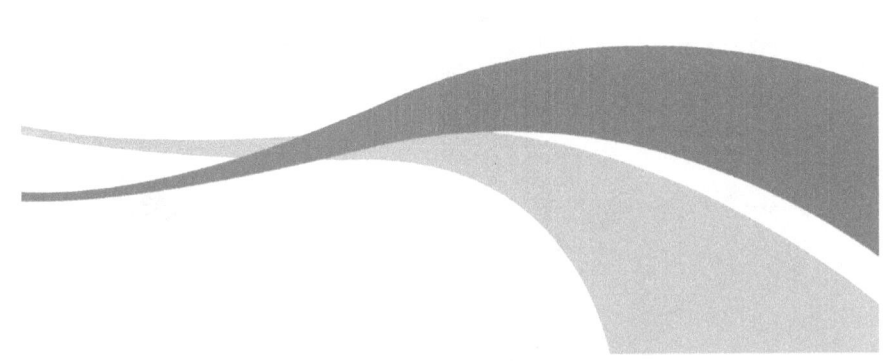

PART 4

WORKPLACE ETIQUETTE

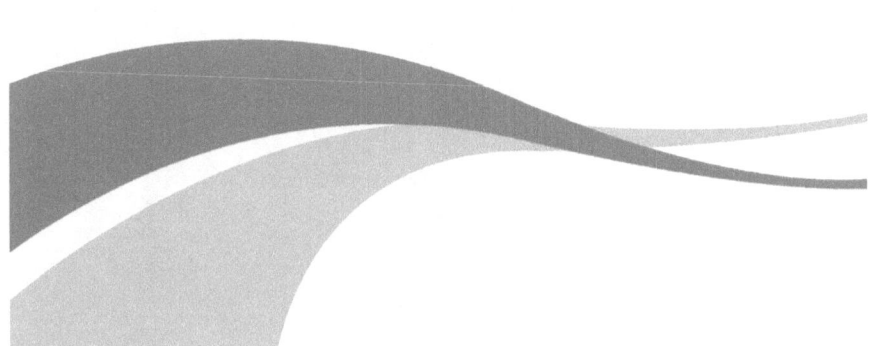

CHAPTER *16*

Work Ethics – Grey Areas or Is It as Clear as Black and White?

Work Ethics – Are there Grey Areas or Is
It as Clear as Black and White?

That poses a question: Is faking being sick a way of getting a well-deserved mental health day, or just a show of bad work ethics?

Calling in Sick

There is such a thing as a mental health day. Though you may not be physically ill, perhaps you need a day to gather your thoughts - which is fine. But if you are getting out of work because you need to finish your holiday shopping, that's not OK.

Also, be mindful of when you are calling in — don't do it when others need you. Call in sick when you have the time, and it will not adversely affect others at the company.

Stealing Office Supplies

An office supplies survey by Career Publisher Vault, Inc. found that 67 percent of employees have taken office supplies from work to use outside the office or for matters unrelated to the job. Stealing physical items, from paper clips to laptops, is an ethical slippery slope. If you're taking the supplies to use for work, that's OK. But, if you're using them for family or personal use, it's not. For example, if you take pads of paper to brainstorm for work during the train ride home, that's fine. But it's not fine to use them to keep track of your kids' soccer game scores or run your side business from home.

"Stealing Time"

The term "stealing time" refers to when you're physically at the office but not actually doing any work. This doesn't mean occasionally checking a personal email address - it's when someone is perpetually checking personal email, always on the phone with friends, or surfing the Internet. There's a social contract that states employees must come to work and actually do their jobs. Just physically being at the office isn't enough to pay a star employee. When work runs out, a good worker doesn't just twiddle his thumbs, but asks for extra assignments.

Coming to Work Sick

Coming in to work with a contagious illness is bad because it makes others sick and prevents them from doing their job. It's also selfish. If you know you could spread your illness to others, stay home for an appropriate amount of time, rest up, and come back to work rejuvenated and healthy.

Spreading Gossip

The number-one workplace ethics violation is being the office gossip, especially if the rumors you spread tend not to be true. Gossiping fosters a negative environment at the office and reduces trust. It's unethical on two levels: it's bad to spread the rumors, and it's bad because of the effect it has on morale.

Everything You Need to Know About Office Spying

Question: Why do companies want to monitor employees' electronic activity in the first place?

Answer: The objective of monitoring systems isn't to "catch" people doing something wrong. It's to try to prevent it from happening in the first place. So, to that end, companies want you to know you're being monitored. The monitoring is a way of saying, "Look, if you do this, we will find out. So, don't do it."

Question: How can I know if my boss is spying on me?

Answer: There's no way to know, but you can assume there's some sort of monitoring going on - most companies do it. While companies are not under any obligation to tell employees they're being monitored - or how they're being monitored - most companies are very up front about it. Read your policy handbook - it's likely in there.

Question: Do I have any rights? Can I go to my employer and say enough is enough, your spying is crossing the line?

Answer: No — you're using the company's computer and it's company property. Your company has the right to monitor the computer and determine the usage of that property.

Question: Should I completely stop using my work computer for personal use?

Answer: For the most part, if you're a strong performer, you can get away with using your computer for some personal matters unless it's in direct violation o company policy; just don't do it too often. Think of it this way: Spend as much time doing personal business on the Web as you would on personal phone calls at work. Would you make a two-hour personal phone call from your desk? You probably would not. Remember, some things are not okay to do ever. Looking at a porn site — even if it's only for a minute — is not okay. A good rule of thumb is: If you wouldn't want your boss to read it, see it, or watch you do it, then avoid these non-work- related activities at work.

CHAPTER 17

How to Agree to Disagree with Your Boss and Keep Your Job

How to Agree to Disagree with Your Boss and Keep Your Job

"Agree to disagree." We have heard this saying so many times, but the question remains: Does it apply to your boss?

It is understood that for every one job opening, there are thousands waiting in line to fill the vacated seat. It is a sensitive time and some companies are taking advantage of this situation by treating their employees any kind of way because they are replaceable by qualified and degreed people. Shame...Shame.

Nonetheless, it should be an unwritten rule that it is okay to agree to disagree. It shows backbone, independent thinking, and a strong will, but don't get too confident or go overboard with agreeing or disagreeing. You don't want to appear to be a "yes" person and you don't want to disagree by arguing or making the boss upset. If you find yourself in this situation, here are a few tips that can open the door of communication and not jeopardize the job:

- Be respectful.
- Prove your point with facts, not opinion or feelings.
- Avoid being emotional. Stay professional.
- No personal attacks or directly putting down the boss's idea.
- Evaluate if you think this battle should be fought or can this one ride?
- Have a clear understanding of your intent to disagree. It must be work-related, not personality differences. You will lose most of the time if it's the latter.
- Your first words will set the tone and the acceptance of your disagreement, so carefully state your intention. Start off with something positive and make sure you let the boss know that you're speaking "with all due respect."
- Only address the key issue. Don't go down memory lane rehashing all of your disagreements. You will set yourself up for failure and the conversation will be over before it gets started.
- Most importantly, take a pulse of your boss. Is your boss becoming defensive, upset, or uninterested? If so, stop for a

minute and reiterate how you like working for the company. Ask if this is a good time for a discussion. Be relaxed and not uptight. Be sincere, not bossy or demanding.

So the answer to the question is yes, you can agree to disagree with your boss. It's your approach, intention, and presentation that will open the ears of the one who can keep you employed.

Remember that to agree to disagree does not mean beating down or arguing with your boss. That will put you in the unemployment line quicker than anything. It means to show intelligence by debating with facts and not opinion. That's what's impressive. Be respectful and prove your point and facts cannot be argued.

CHAPTER *18*

The Seven Deadly Sins
of Office Romance

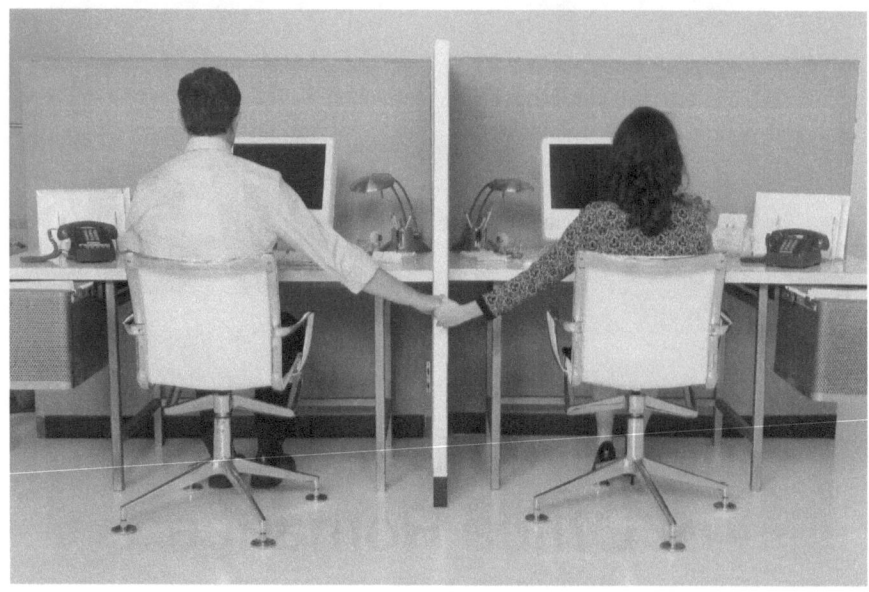

The Seven Deadly Sins of Office Romance

Amore…Love…Romance…It can strike at any time, without warning, bewildering you with sudden, primal urges, flooding you with fantasies and daydreams. It can be an instantaneous attraction or move with the slow, burning rhythm of a tango. It's the first dance invented that you didn't need to be taught and the oldest Golden Oldie that everybody knows all the words to the song. Poets have immortalized it as an element as potent as fire or wind. Al Green moans about "Something that can make you do wrong / make you do right," and we all know what he's talking about. We're smitten. We know it can happen anywhere, too. It can happen at school, at the supermarket, at a garage sale, and at work.

When Venus and Mars connect on the job, the rules for romance change. Acting on the most natural impulses can brand you as a champion of fate ("We're meant to be together"). Or, if you're not careful, you'll be seen as an unrepentant and unemployable sinner.

Not long ago the idea of mixing professional business with personal pleasure was considered taboo, a literal kiss-of-death to your career. Large companies have barred employees from dating, and marriage was out of the question. Under the old rules, Microsoft Corporation Chief,

Bill Gates, would have been called on the carpet for dating Melinda French, a coworker, whom he later married.

By the 1990s, the stigma had nearly vanished. Partly because we all know someone, or we ourselves, have crisscrossed career and Cupid. In a 1998 poll, conducted by the American Management Association, over 80 percent of the surveyed group, mostly mid-level managers, said they knew of or had been involved in an office romance.

The temperatures in the offices have soared. With the thermostat blazing red, the questions and attitudes have become more complex. It's too hot to wear full-fledged armor, and foolish to streak through this scorcher half-naked. There are as many opinions about how to handle it as there are theories on UFO sightings. There's definitely something out there (or in here), and it's touched down in the nerve center of the office, from the smallest mom and pop establishment to the White House.

The scandal in the "Big House" gave us all pause. After the media hounded us for a year with the lurid details of "Our former President Bill and intern Monica close encounters," as if it were a serialized version of the Jerry Springer Show, the aftershock was clearly a heightened awareness of workplace liaisons and their impact. The President's definition of what constitutes "sex" may differ from that of most American adults, but that there is "romance" at the office is indisputable and actually reflects a common occurrence in the work culture: One out of three Americans have dated a coworker.

A study conducted by The Families and Work Institute of New York found that over one-third of all relationships began on the job. Surprisingly, over 45 percent of these couples become long-term committed relationships or marriages. A separate study by the Society of Human Resource Management confirmed these findings, with 55 percent of 617 professionals reporting that marriage was the "most likely outcome" of an office romance. Singles' bars, the gym, the church, and even the personal ads have all taken a backseat to the one inevitable place people meet their significant other: across the cubicle.

Still waiting to exhale? Some cautionary advice: Don't hold your breath. You can meet your one and only and glide through the minefield of office amore unscratched. But living your love life on the job can damage your credibility, create an environment of discord, and even find you in the litigious nightmare of sexual harassment suits. Being a minority can color perceptions of your professionalism. You're under a different code of scrutiny. Double standards of sexual mores regarding women may appear more subdued, but they're not extinct.

In the time it takes to steal a kiss (which you think nobody notices), protocol, professional conduct, and privacy can converge into a three-headed monster which feeds on the raw meat of your love-swelled heart. How much of your private life remains private if you date from the company pool? What happens when it doesn't work out? What about office gossip and performance reviews? Can you expect to be taken seriously if you're sleeping through the company's phone directory? What's the difference between ardent pursuit and harassment? Do you keep it a secret? When should you tell?

So, before a subtle wink turns into full-fledged wooing, avoid the following mistakes...the deadliest of office romance sins. If you're flying high on the endorphins of love and about to jump out of the plane, check your parachute. The love craft could experience turbulence and take a nosedive, so don't wing it. Ignorance is unforgivable.

1. SLOTH

You didn't find out your company's policies.

You can't resist. You've both agreed to see each other. After magnetism comes management of your relationship. Whether the budding bloom is still fresh with dew or about to be pressed into the pages of a serious chapter, you need to find out what your company's policy is regarding inter-office dating. This can be tricky. There is no one-size-fits-all standard plan.

Most companies use a system of benign neglect. A "we won't ask, so you don't tell" approach. Strategic Outsourcing reported in a 1997 study of 592 companies that over 90 percent did not have a written policy on employee dating. This lack of policy alone causes problems. Dennis M. Powers, author of *The Office Romance: Playing with Fire Without Getting Burned* (AMA-COM Books), agrees. "This leaves too much to an individual manager's discretion. By not having a formal office romance policy, employees and supervisors alike don't know the rules and this creates dangerous waters."

If your company doesn't have a formal policy, the next best thing is to try and gauge the general attitudes about romantic fraternizing. If the other employees and management have a laissez-faire approach and your performance is rated more important than whom you go home with, chances are the relationship won't become an issue. That's the best-case scenario. A worse case is a complete misinterpretation and worse still, if there are not any clear-cut policies, then the door swings wide open for sexual harassment suits. You can't be slothful here. Find out.

2. MEDDLING, GOSSIP, SABOTAGE

Can I get a Witness? It's often said "love is blind." That statement is true only to those who are smitten. Check your peripheral vision. Cupid can strike you deaf, dumb, and demoted. When it comes to your coworkers and your manager, they have X-ray vision and supernatural powers. The walls have ears, eyes, and a very big mouth. If you think your affair is a secret, think again. Mutual attraction between men and women can be hidden for a while, but not for very long. You don't have to admit to anything. The people around you can sense the energy. Couples in swoon radiate a tremendous amount of sexual energy. Your coworkers might revel in your joy. Some will go full-throttle on envy; sabotage is the next step, right before the quicksand.

Remember, your newfound bliss has a wide radius. It affects the dynamics of the office, and your peers are human beings first, coworkers second. Envy shows up as gossip-mongering, rumors, and straight-out lies about you. If there's any hint of favoritism toward you or your beloved, the seeds of envy are planted. Can't prevent the fallout, but you should be attuned. Envy is a strong motivator. Best advice: prevention. At the office your lover is a coworker first, sweetheart second, third, or fourth.

3. ANGER

When the Relationship Doesn't Work Out: Maurice and Cynthia, Romance Gone Awry.

It started with the look and ended with a "look out!" En route to the fax machine, 33-year-old budding architect Maurice did a double take as he passed a cubicle with a new and very pretty occupant sorting through back issues of Architectural Digest. Later, in a staff meeting, Maurice was thrilled when the department head introduced "Cynthia" as his new research assistant. Shaking hands, they held a smile just a bit longer than customary and exchanged that look. A spark. Unmistakable interest and chemistry. They started dating – secretly. Oblivious to office gossip and rumors of favoritism, they moved in together.

Before the year was over, they split up, and it wasn't pretty.

Cynthia threw all of Maurice's clothes out the window and flushed his car keys down the toilet. He confronted her at work. A screaming match ensued. Evil email volleys were lobbed back and forth. The look became a glare of contempt. Maurice moved on to another relationship— the latest receptionist. To top it off, another employee who had worked in the same office with them filed a claim of hostile work environment.

Management had a solution: Fire both of them.

Maurice and Cynthia could have been spared the corporate rod if they were lawyers on the hit comedy "Ally McBeal", where the edgy triangle of Love-Rejection-and-Jealousy on the job doesn't include messy endings where people get the pink slip. In the real world, working with the one you love isn't 43 minutes of neatly-packaged farce you can click off with the remote.

The story dramatizes how volatile a situation can become when fusing matters of the heart with work. Anger, pure unfiltered anger, can slip through the fissure of a breakup and explode with exacting clarity. The way to avoid these flare-ups is to create a clear exit plan for the relationship. In other words, Maurice and Cynthia didn't consider what the consequences would be if their relationship failed, or how they would continue working together. Love fights, bickering, and his verbal assaults are all completely inappropriate behavior. On company time, your personal issues are a hindrance to productivity. Although we don't enter relationships with divorce in mind, when you co-mingle the elements of love and work, you must evaluate all possible outcomes and how you will handle it. Management was right.

4. GREED

Coming Out Too Soon - Abusing Company Time/Privileges

Did you tell your office mate you're dating the guy in accounting? Oh, and you've only gone out, say, twice? When the relationship is on track, then you tell, never before. Are you six months into something rock-solid and you think your co-workers should make allowances, or excuses, for your late lunches and hushed inter-office phone calls to your significant other? Are you coming in late, punching out early, or missing deadlines? Did your relationship have a bad day and you're moody and preoccupied? Has the ebb and flow of your love affair become the center of your work universe?

Greed can become an ugly thing. You've been privileged already. And you want more. Somebody has to pick up the slack, and apparently it's not you and you don't care. If Cupid has convinced you that you deserve more on the job, you've got it all wrong. Greed swiftly morphs into arrogance, and that vanity doesn't produce the same results. You'll be off the team, pronto.

5. GLUTTONY

Playing Relationship Roulette

"Those pretty wrongs that liberty commits..." Shakespeare could have been writing about Amin, who never met a coworker he didn't date. In the course of two years, Amin developed a reputation as a Roving Romeo sowing wild oats in the company soil. Not only did he play Casanova to women in four departments, he dated them simultaneously. When his company transferred him to another city, he began the march all over again. One woman resisted his charms. He pursued. She informed her supervisor. Her supervisor checked the corporate branch human resources department. "What about this Amin?", Amin's former boss was questioned. Yes, there were some complaints about him. The woman sued for harassment and won.

This behavior is nothing less than treating the workplace like a playpen or your own personal dating service. Gluttons only date their coworkers. They think the staff is a Whitman's Sampler of chocolates: they need to pinch each one to see what's inside. These people are binge eaters; anything in the cupboard (office) will do. A reputation like this can follow you around like a foul smell, for years. You'll be knee deep in it, while someone bangs your head with the shovel at the next meeting for Recovering Office Romance Addicts – 12 steppers with resumes reeking of lawsuits.

6. LUST

Breaking the rules of discretion/disrespecting boundaries.

This sin should be easy to avoid, but it's usually the first one committed.

There's a distinct difference between flirting and insisting. The motto should be: If it isn't a clear yes, take it as a no. There's an added psychological variable we should look at here. Men and women share some of the same call-and-response buttons of the sexual dance. Traditionally, men have taken the role of "pursuer." He needs to win the woman. He needs to "dance" for her, so to speak. That's what pursuit, or better, courting is all about. The woman traditionally responds to these entreaties with rebuffs, coy behavior, all subtle hints that she's in the dance, too. It's part of the excitement of meeting someone of attraction. The dance means nothing without a measure of resistance, and men are tuned in to this. So, an initial "not interested" can read like a "maybe" to a man; he's used to reading between the lines. It very well could be just that, "Maybe, we'll see." When this dance is played out on the job, the risks of misinterpretation are high. It's a delicate area and can become inflamed with lightning speed. Sexual innuendoes, suggestiveness, touching, and gazing are hazards at the office.

The common definition of sexual harassment is behavior which "has the purpose and effect of substantially interfering with an individual's work performance or creating an intimidating, hostile, or offensive working environment." Read that twice and take a large dose of vitamin "D" - as in discretion.

It should go without saying that sex at the office is a bad idea. Period.

7. PRIDE

Dating your boss/subordinate.

Be prepared to quit or relocate. This is like drinking and driving. If the relationship is consensual, not love-at-first-sight…, if the powers that be are not particularly horrified, and if the parties are respectful, discrete and professional, believe it or not, most companies turn a blind eye. Yet, given such liberalism, dating inside a reporting relationship can be a disaster waiting to happen. Since these generally involve a male supervisor and female subordinate, the atmosphere is ripe for legal action. Supervisors are harder to replace and the corporate world is not democratic: the least-valued employee is the first fired. If a company consistently boots the woman, it opens itself up to sex discrimination suits.

Pride can delude you into believing your conduct is above scrutiny and that you're invulnerable. You should have learned the lesson when you passed through *lust*.

CHAPTER 19

Think Twice Before You Recommend a Friend

Think Twice Before You Recommend a Friend

So, you want to refer a friend? Even though it seems like a small favor in a tough job market, it's important to move carefully before recommending a friend to someone in your professional network. Referring a friend to a former colleague or someone in your network is simple for most people, but if your friend is less than stellar at the job, it may backfire on your own career. Because you know your friends mostly from a social perspective, vouching for them on the job may affect your credibility.

<u>Consider the following:</u>

Referring someone whom you've met just a few times or haven't been in contact with in years could be risky. Before you press "send" and pass on a resume, evaluate what you know about the person and how that person acts in the workplace. Do you know the person well enough to recommend to your employer, or any other company for that matter?

Find out as much as you can about your friend's employment history before sending out a recommendation. Think about it objectively before making a decision. Don't refer the friend if your friend's general employment history is spotty for reasons you know to be negative. Should your friend get a negative reputation on the job, it could put you in an uncomfortable position.

Even if you casually want to put your friend in touch with a current or former boss, this could result in the company's asking for a formal referral. Consider whether you'd want the employer to contact you concerning your friend. It's easy to empathize with a job seeker, but formally vouching for skills on the job is a more serious decision.

Sometimes there are other more personal reasons for asking that your name not be mentioned. Your own reputation at the company or with a former boss can influence how your recommendation is perceived. Your friend may be better off pursuing the job on his own. So, even if you're totally positive about your friend, recommending him may still not be your best bet.

If you decide to allow your friends to use your name in the interview, only let them mention your name. If the interviewer asks how did you find this company or how did you know the employee, tell your friend to make it short and sweet. Avoid any 'Best Friends Forever (BFF)' conversations with the interviewer. What also needs to be taken into consideration is the fact that sometimes mentioning that you know a person already in the workplace might be counterproductive. Some employers may not want 'friends' working together.

Another reason to be cautious of referring a friend, especially if you are a manager or supervisor, is the potential of other employees feeling any resentment. Maybe someone else in the department wanted that job, but you did not recommend them.

Before making a recommendation or taking a job that surfaced due to a friend's recommendation, think about how it will reflect your working relationship down the road. Avoid telling others if you get the job. Keep a low profile of any friendship or family relationship. First earn your worth and respect from others by your skills.

Most important, before passing on a friend's resume, think carefully about how it will affect your career. Also, make it known to your friend that a referral from you does not mean a guaranteed job position.

CHAPTER 20

How to Turn a Bad Annual Review Around

How to Turn a Bad Annual Review Around

It's a simple truth that no one likes being judged and very few like being critiqued. That natural disdain is what makes the formal job-review process nerve-wracking for many. The idea of sitting across from your supervisor as your achievements and shortcomings are laid out in front of you on a stark sheet of paper can be an intimidating one. What makes the occurrence more daunting is that far too many employees walk into the process blindly. If they've managed to avoid any major screw-ups during the course of the year and haven't been chewed out by the boss, then it's safe to assume they're doing a good job, right? Wrong.

"No communication is not the same as good communication," stressed Lynn Avitabile, managing director and global head of human resources for JPMorgan Chase's Global Asset Management (No. 25 on The DiversityInc Top 50 Companies for Diversity list). "If they're not telling you you're doing OK, maybe they also are not informing you if you're not meeting expectations."

The worst time to find out you're not pulling your weight is during the annual review. Indeed, human resource executives stress that the best way to avoid this is by taking control of your review process and monitoring your progress throughout the year.

"The mistake people make about performance reviews is that they treat them as if they were being done to them. You should never treat an evaluation that way because, if you do, you're giving the other guy carte blanche power to determine how you're doing," said Avitabile. "The one rule to make sure performance evaluations work is to take a hugely active part in evaluating your own performance."

"One way to remove the mystery is to make sure it's a yearlong, ongoing process," noted Bet Franzone, a spokesperson for American Express (No. 22 on The DiversityInc Top 50 Companies for Diversity list).

At American Express, Franzone said, "Every employee, from customer-service representatives to executive managers, goes through a number of evaluation processes throughout the year as part of a company-wide performance-management process."

"It's a critical factor in helping our employees manage their performance. Our process occurs year-round to maximize individual performance, and it involves future goal-setting, ongoing assessment of work against goals, and an annual review," she said.

The company's review process consists of goal-setting at the beginning of the year with each employee to maximize individual performance. During the course of the year, there is an ongoing assessment of how those goals are being met. For some departments, this also includes a mid-year review. The process culminates with a year-end sit-down with a supervisor to identify ongoing development and leadership opportunities.

"It's a top-to-bottom approach. So, goals are set at the executive level and those are cascaded down throughout the organization so people can set their goals based on their responsibilities. The system is designed to clarify the expectations so there is no ambiguity," said Franzone. "We have very clearly defined competencies of what constitutes high performance, so there are very clear models employees can use to help develop their performance. The system is designed so the employee is never in the dark.

"It's the fear of the unknown, of finding out what your boss is really thinking about you and your performance, that makes the process so untenable for many," replied Avitabile.

Avitabile has worked for the same supervisor at JPMorgan for the last 10 years. She makes a point of sitting down with the supervisor on a monthly basis to discuss performance issues and to make sure their mutual goals are being accomplished. She's broken their meetings into designated categories. One is the 'business as usual' segment, which consists of reviewing weekly reports or other areas where there won't be large variations from month to month. "The second bracket consists of those things that are strategic deliverables for this month or this year, and to let let my boss know how I'm prioritizing them," she said. This gives her ample opportunity for critical face time with her boss and provides her with an opening to request any additional resources she might require to accomplish her tasks. "Send e-mails. Send written memos. Do whatever is necessary to keep that communication open and flowing," she urged. "If you send clearly-outlined details of what you're working on, the timeframes you're dealing with and the resources you're using, and then you deliver, then how can I give you a bad review?" asked Avitabile.

But if you do find yourself in the unfortunate position of being on the wrong end of a bad review, there are some steps to take before packing your bags and brushing off your resume.

"Too often, an employee's first reaction is to begin looking for another job," said Avitabile. "The first thing you have to do is go to your supervisor without any defensiveness and be willing to listen absolutely to what they have to say. Then tell them you were really surprised and you would love to get some help understanding what happened and how you can turn it around."

Most people, believes Avitabile, are "conflict-avoiders." So, when supervisors are put in the unenviable position of delivering critical feedback to a subordinate, they're often as uncomfortable as the person on the receiving end. "But if they've done it, you have to get them to feel like you can take it, listen to it and learn from it," she said. "If they perceive you are coming to them to argue, they will simply shut down." So, ask your supervisor to be as specific as possible in the areas where it's determined you fell short. The goal is to walk away with enough information to recover and rebound from the review. "You have to know enough to know what to fix," said Avitabile.

Responding positively even in the face of harsh criticism sends a message that you're willing to work on your flaws and correct them, if possible. By demonstrating you're committed to improving yourself and open to being critiqued, without getting negative or paranoid, your supervisor is apt to feel more confident in giving you the information you'll need to improve. "The reason most people fall off the career wagon is because people don't really tell them what they really think about them," said Avitabile.

But the goal is to avoid the dilemma altogether by actively owning your own performance evaluation. Most employees should assume the best management they're going to get over the course of their career is the management that they are going to give themselves. "No one will care about your career progression more than you will," said Avitabile. "You should never give away things that are of the most importance to you."

CHAPTER 21

Workplace Drama
- Stay Away!

Workplace Drama - Stay away!

You've heard the phrase "Drama Momma". On the job, it means conflict, so stay away!

Not so fast gentlemen, this means you, too.

There is nothing worse than getting caught up in workplace drama. If you want to keep a clean image and a professional reputation, stay as far away as you can from people who enjoy drama on the job. Conflict, jealousy, and gossip equal disaster.

Many who engage in such acts are generally bored with life, envious, or out to sabotage someone's reputation. They are generally unhappy or hostile individuals out to make everyone else's life miserable. If you find yourself caught up in this drama, you will also find yourself in the same pitiful position, and maybe even out of a job.

Just remember, there is no positive outcome in office drama, so run! Competition is healthy in the workplace, but drama is not.

Do not taint your image by getting involved or even hanging out with a drama king or queen. This may be difficult, especially if you are the target. See the circumstance for what it is and stay professional. It can sneak up on you, so be aware of who enjoys stirring up trouble and then sitting back and watching the show. It is really not difficult to identify this person; he/she usually has established a reputation. However, be careful how you handle workplace drama or you may find yourself as an outcast by default.

Here are ways to avoid it and keep your status intact and reputation clean:

- When you find yourself engaged in a conversation with the drama king or queen, make the conversation general. Never focus on an individual or feed the negative tone.
- When the conversation begins to turn into a gossip column, gracefully close the conversation by getting back to work or turn the conversation into something positive. For example, "Did you hear that Betty is up for a promotion when she just got the job?" You can reply by saying, "Wow, that says a lot about

the company and that management is willing to recognize hard work. That could be you or me some day and wouldn't that be great?"

- If you are being harassed via email by the person who wants to create drama in the workplace, be sure to save the emails written to you and, if you must respond, be brief and to the point. For example, you can state that you would love to talk, but you are working on a project. Or, state that you would prefer that management handle the issue. Or, mention that using company time to email non-related work would not be beneficial to either of you. Sometimes avoiding the emails will not work, which could cause conflict and tension among you and that person, which could create drama in the workplace. So address the issue professionally, but keep the emails in case you are ever accused of stirring up conflict.

- With this said, it is important not to, however, encourage the person to talk to you about any office drama. Just let them know that you come to work to work and not to get involved in any office politics. Be polite and smile as you say it.

- When you see a circle of people, go the other way. Do not get trapped into joining the circle, which looks like a witch hunt. Instead, if invited, mention that you must get back to work and you'll talk with them later. Remember it is not enough just to avoid the trouble-maker, but you must stay friendly and keep your distance.

- Stay stern and confident. Never let them see you sweat. Avoid a situation that has a potentially negative outcome. You are not being wimpy, but smart. Do not let your pride get in the way of turning the other cheek or refocusing. You are trying to keep your reputation intact and a paycheck coming in the mail.

- Let people say what they want to say, but document any written comments that might be negative towards you if you are the target. Never confront the drama person who is stirring the pot; instead keep your distance, work professionally, and, if necessary, bring it to the boss's attention. Reassure the boss that you are here to do a job and that you are focused on achieving the company goals.

Since a "Drama King and Queen" exist at every job, it is best to know how to deal with the person. However, if you fit this shoe, get it together. Leave the drama out of the workplace; use that energy to better yourself and to get ahead on the job.

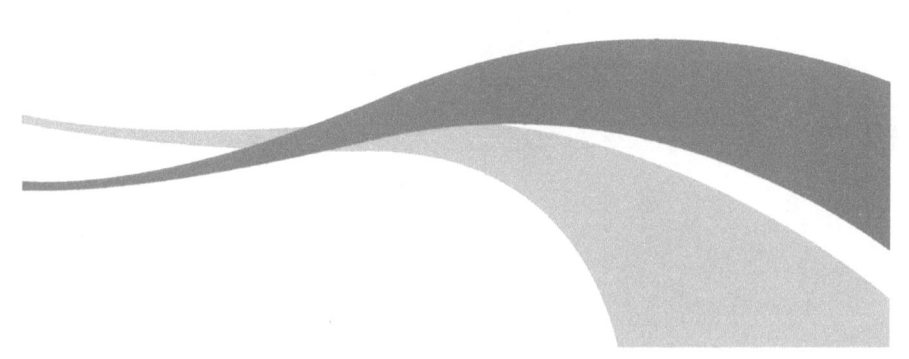

PART 5

RE-ENTRY INTO THE JOB MARKET

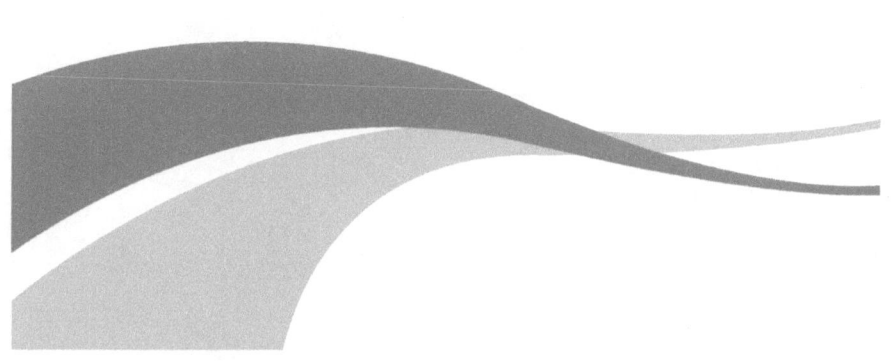

CHAPTER 22

Volunteering Your Way to a Paid Position

Calvin Lovick & Angela M. Cranon-Charles, M.A.

Volunteering Your Way to a Paid Position

Millions of Americans volunteer a portion of their time each year, from donating a few hours weekly to nearby hospitals to participating in breast cancer walks to raise research funds. Many people contribute both time and skills to a variety of organizations and causes. But if you've lost your job and are thinking of abandoning your volunteer commitments, outplacement executives say, "Don't. Volunteering can be both psychologically and strategically helpful to your job change effort." Whether you are looking for your first job, wanting to change careers, re-entering the workforce, or are just in between jobs, volunteering can help you land that next paycheck. This is the one step people can do to get their foot in the door. The time commitment is flexible and being a volunteer looks good on a resume.

Not only will you enjoy the satisfaction of helping a worthy cause, you will gain valuable work experience and show employers you have initiative and motivation. Employers are often interested in well-rounded people who have interests outside of their career. Whether you are paid or unpaid, volunteering counts as work experience.

Volunteering will allow you to fill gaps in your resume when you are out of work and will ease the isolation you may feel with trying to find a job.

Volunteering also helps you to build your network. You will have a chance to meet the organization's representatives as well as other volunteers who may have leads to job vacancies at their own companies. Select a volunteer position that requires you to speak or greet the guests in some way. This will enable people to notice you without any special overdone actions.

"A long job search can be demoralizing. Volunteering, on the other hand, helps people regain their energy and enthusiasm," said Joy Childs, who has nearly 25 years of experience heading human resources departments at a variety of companies. "Volunteering can put job hunters in a better, more positive frame of mind. It gives them a chance to give back something of value, since too often, when people lose their jobs, they feel as if they've also lost their value." Childs added,

"Volunteering at a time when employers don't seem to need you provides a psychological boost and a feeling that you are needed and appreciated by the organizations and individuals your volunteer work impacts."

On the other hand, despite the benefits of volunteering, Childs tells job hunters it's a mistake to use volunteering to avoid job hunting. "It's critical for job hunters to maintain a balance and make sure they're putting substantial time and effort into their job search efforts," she said.

Lena Cole Dennis, who has an extensive background working with local nonprofits, agrees, and stresses the value of taking time to volunteer while job hunting. "Career management professionals commonly urge unemployed people to make job hunting a full-time, 40-hour a week job," she said. "I agree, it's critical to treat job hunting as a job when you're unemployed, but I'd recommend people do an effective 35-hour a week search - and use the other hours to do activities like volunteering that makes them feel good. The sense of purpose and satisfaction people get from helping others can help overcome the disappointments of the job search process."

Looking beyond the psychological benefits of volunteering, it also has its strategic benefits for job hunters. Volunteering is a great way for job hunters to expand their contacts - and many job opportunities come to people as a result of their personal contacts. Even for jobs advertised in newspapers or posted online, people can often find something that matches their skills.

Volunteering can lead to paid jobs with the same organizations. Job hunters intentionally trying to change careers can also find volunteering valuable. A successful sales professional who wants to pursue a professional fundraising career, for example, can volunteer to coordinate a fundraiser for a non-profit organization he/she supports supports. That volunteer role could bolster your chances when you are interviewing for a paid fundraising job because it could demonstrate your success in this profession.

When choosing a place to volunteer, experts suggest you think carefully about what you want and select the organization that best suits your needs. Consider an organization that will offer you skills or experience you lack. You can choose a national organization such as the Urban League, United Way, the American Red Cross, United

Negro College Fund, or Habitat for Humanity, or you can look to your community hospitals, animal shelters, youth centers, community centers, museums, soup kitchens, prisons, and sports teams.

For those looking for their first job in the high-tech or computer industry, consider grassroots environmental groups, homeless shelters, churches, and other nonprofit organizations that often rely on technology professionals or professionals-to-be to do everything from setting up local area networks to developing websites. Though it's not a guaranteed way to overcome having no professional experience, volunteering is a valuable way to prove yourself outside the classroom. It can also help you make the contacts essential to a successful job search.

It's great hands-on experience and it looks good on a resume. The work can build technology skills and also people skills. It's also showing that you can see things through to completion. That's just what employers want to know when they've got an applicant who is self-taught or newly trained. Can the applicant work on a team? Can he/she handle deadlines? Does he/she know how to translate classroom lessons to the workplace? Volunteer work provides answers to those questions, and can also provide key references to secure future employment. Techies looking for volunteer opportunities should check into volunteer-matching services in the local area. See examples at techsoup.org. Also, go to community volunteer centers that coordinate volunteer opportunities. Call the city, county, or Chamber of Commerce to find the appropriate contacts. Or, create your own volunteer assignment. If you're already associated with a particular organization, suggest a tech-related project you can handle.

Eight Steps to Successful Volunteering

Step One

Check with the local, county, city, and state websites to see what upcoming opportunities there are for assisting with projects and events.

Step Two

Check the local media outlets to see what the buzz is on events with dignitaries present. This could have a great impact on your employment prospects.

Step Three

Check with people you know already to see what networking events they are attending. They may have opportunities for you to assist in planning or actively working the event. This could bring freebies and fringe benefits. Perhaps, this could mean a free meal or gift which you would normally not get. In addition, this provides the chance to rub elbows and exchange contact information.

Step Four

Select a volunteer position that requires you to speak or greet the guests in some way. This will enable people to notice you without any special overdone actions.

Step Five

Be ready to collect contact information. Also, have a small pocket or purse for ladies available.

Step Six

Volunteer and speak to the people who organized the event before and after it begins. Make small talk before leaving to get their attention and to hopefully have them make note of you and the conversation.

Step Seven

Send an email or call within 48 hours of meeting your top five contacts at the event. This should always include the people who can benefit you the most and those who made it possible for you to be there. For instance, contact the organizer of the event to thank them as you express interest in assisting in their future events.The top five should receive a short simple email, or phone call, that explains who you are, and you should end with the discussion about something's being done in the future - for example, meet for lunch sometime soon, share information on a topic, setting a time to talk later, etc.

Step Eight

Get ready to tell people about yourself and share your contact information. Think of this as a relationship that can turn into a job. This informal method will get you through the tough economic times.

Warnings for Volunteers

- Be patient when it comes to networking.
- Always organize the contacts as soon as possible and write down something distinctive about them for recall purposes.
- Pick events and projects that include fringe benefits to make the time more enjoyable.
- Always ask about parking facilities, reimbursement for gas, and where to meet specifically for the day of an event. Get the complete contact information of the organizer or team leader.
- Expect some last-minute changes in the event.
- Do not gossip.

CHAPTER 23

How to Successfully
Re-enter the Job Market

How to Successfully Re-enter the Job Market

What is the biggest obstacles a person experiences re-entering the job market today?

According to most career counselors, being relevant and up-to-date in your particular field is the most common hurdle to overcome. With technology moving so fast, many skills and knowledge are outdated every couple of years. *What should you do to reconnect yourself?* The first step is to take some brush-up courses prior to beginning the job search. Research the field or industry you want to enter. Check out any recent legislation or news articles that address changes affecting your industry. That way, when you sit down for an interview, you are abreast of current news about the industry.

Visit the library or bookstore to do research. Find out what refresher courses are offered by professional organizations, local colleges, and adult education programs. Brushing up takes time, so it helps to start thinking about your return to the work force well in advance. The key to re-entering the workforce successfully is having skills that will give you an edge in the marketplace. You may need to brush up on rusty skills or acquire some new ones. For example, being computer literate is very important in many of today's jobs. If you do not have a background that includes using a computer, you may want to look into taking a computer course.

Begin reviewing your previous work experience and listing the skills you've acquired on earlier jobs. Then take a look at what you've done during your years away from the job market. Remember, all experience counts, whether you were paid for it or not. Think about the skills you use at home, with volunteer work, or hobbies. Then consider how they can be applied to a new job. Once you've listed your experience and skills, think about the type of work you want to pursue. Compare the skills you may need for the job with the skills you currently have. There will probably be some gaps, but now is the time to fill in those gaps, even before you begin your job search.

Here is a quick summary of information you need to know and follow when re-entering the job market.

- **Know specifically the career you want:**

What would I enjoy doing all day? What career could I wake up to each day? How happy will I be going to work? Will I be satisfied with the salary?

- **Know your talents and skills:**

There is a difference between what you like to do and what you actually can do. Know your expertise, qualities, talent and skills by testing them out. Do people compliment you on your work? How well do you perform your talents? Are you passionate about your talents and skills and know that you do them well?

- **Don't be shy. Display all of your skills in your resume, and especially in your Curriculum Vitae:**

Always include your work experience as well as volunteer work. It takes a certain kind of person to volunteer his/her time to a cause. For this reason, all that you do should be revealed either in a cover letter, a resume, or a Curriculum Vitae.

- **Internships should not go unnoticed:**

Internships can be an important step towards the job of your dreams, especially if you work in the field of your chosen career. For this reason, any internship should be taken very seriously, as though you were getting paid a million bucks. This is an opportunity to do a little bit of everything. Find the job you want to do as a career, then make sure that you tailor your internship to represent some of the same skills. Intern at the company you may want to work for in the long run. Many times interns are hired, especially those with degrees.

- **Networking is not overrated:**

Join organizations, attend networking business meetings, and socialize where business people hang out. These are not just social gatherings, but opportunities to network and to get to know people who are working where you want to start a career. That one event could lead to a lifelong career. Sitting in front of a computer could never replace the craft of networking with the right people.

CHAPTER 24

A Resignation Letter That Won't Burn Bridges

A Resignation Letter That Won't Burn Bridges

As much as a person might want to leave a job, one of the hardest things to do is resign. It does not come easy, especially when butterflies are fluttering in the stomach and sweaty palms reveal the eagerness to approach a supervisor when giving a two-week's notice.

There is no getting around this process; therefore, it is essential to exit professionally and without burning any bridges. The consequences of leaving a job with a distasteful resignation letter could be detrimental to a career in the long run.

For this reason, putting together a well-written and thought-out resignation letter is needed. If you are leaving a job because your boss is difficult to work with, remember, nothing stays the same. One day at the same company management could change, and, if you want to return, your file will include this professional resignation letter. If you do not give a two-week's notice or leave without providing a resignation letter, the consequences will fall on you, not your boss.

Another reason to provide a resignation letter is that you may run into your old boss on your next job where he/she may be the supervisor, or possibly worse, a potential client. The lack of a resignation letter or bad-mouthing the boss would ruin this relationship and possibly result in a loss of income.

Relationships are important, even if two people are at odds with each other. Sometimes the conflict is not the clash between two people, but the environment in which the two worked. So, in a different environment, the same two people might have a better relationship and can work together. Careers are built on connections and networking, so writing a positive resignation letter to someone you may not particularly care to work with would be beneficial in the long run. In return, you may receive a good reference letter from this ex-employer.

How To Write A Resignation Letter:

The resignation letter should not be personal or imply jabs that your boss is the reason you might be leaving. It should praise what good was found in the supervisor and the company and indicate how tough it was to make the decision to leave. The boss must indicate to his boss the reason someone is leaving the department, and, of course, he would not want to take any blame for your leaving.

Don't use the resignation letter to place blame or to point out all of the wrongs in the department or the company; instead, keep it simple and set aside personal feelings, so that your leaving of the company will not put a negative mark on your profile.

The resignation letter should include:

- Show your appreciation for having the opportunity to work at the company.
- Personally thank the supervisor.
- Explain the reason you are leaving, but stay positive, e.g., an opportunity that would lead to a career more focused on your interest or the job is a promotion from what you currently hold.
- At all costs, avoid any negative comments, even if you have a lump in your throat. Not pointing out the obvious that your boss is aware of might change his attitude about you, or at least show how professional you really are in an unpleasant situation.

Example of a resignation letter:

Although the following will provide you with some tips on what to include in a resignation letter, Googling "Resignation Letter Samples" will give you a host of examples to follow. NEVER, NEVER, however, cut and paste any exact letter from the Internet, as it can easily be discovered that you have done so. Instead, follow the guidelines that will allow you to write an effective resignation letter:

- Address the letter specifically to the person or persons whom you need to notify that you are resigning.
- In the header be sure to specifically put: Letter of Resignation.
- Make the letter brief, but long enough to leave on a positive note.

- Make sure you let the supervisor know that you will have your work in order for the next person to come aboard with a smooth transition.
- Be sure to praise and thank the "important" people in writing. This will go a long way.

Keep in mind that this letter will stay in your files for years to come and, if you ever re-apply to work for this company, there will be something to look back on that would be considered a professional and positive exit from the company.

CHAPTER 25

Do Job Fairs Really Pay Off?

Do Job Fairs Really Pay Off?

How many job fairs do you attend a year? You probably do not attend enough. Job fairs can be wonderful and resourceful tools when looking for a new career. Most allow registration via the Internet; others are just walk-in registrations. Job fairs can also be beneficial to those who don't really know what career they want to pursue or are re-entering the job market - for example, a student, someone changing careers, or the unemployed.

Attending job fairs also allows the attendee to learn more about corporations and what they have to offer. It gives you a chance to meet some of the personnel who might be key players in the hiring process for the company.

Additionally, job fairs are a one-stop job hunting venue to hit multiple opportunities at one given time. If you're relocating, finding out when job fairs are being held in the city of choice would allow you to possibly land a job sooner than looking at the wanted ads.

Although attending a job fair is one important aspect of discovering hidden employment treasures, another important factor is being prepared when you go. A one-on-one interview at a company is not any different than sitting at a booth talking to a person face-to-face at a job fair. Therefore, you must:

- Look the part. Dress in business attire.
- Take plenty of professional-looking resumes.
- Take a generic cover letter stating what position you're seeking.
- If required, take samples of your work or a portfolio.
- Mark on the back of the hiring company's business card the date and location of the job fair, and the person you spoke with, just in case they call or you need to contact them. You have a record of your meeting.
- Keep the collection of business cards and company literature organized so that you can follow up on any leads.

- Take a business card of your own, even if you are not currently employed, which should include your name, contact information, and your specialty. This might impress them.

Sometimes the company personnel will take more than a resume and sometimes they will not, especially if they are traveling a distance. You might have to email additional material to them. Remember, there could be hundreds attending the job fair at the same time you are, so make a lasting impression by being professional and prepared.

CHAPTER 26

Using Social Networking to Re-Enter the Job Market in the 21st Century

Using Social Networking to Re-Enter the
Job Market in the 21st Century

You're unemployed, underemployed or just want a career change, so in the 21st century you are trying to find a job. Very few businesses actually want candidates walking to the office to fill out an application. Today, the job search starts on the computer. It is called DIGITAL NETWORKING. This is the preferred method, and sometimes the only way, to actually reach out to companies or to even apply for a job. Digital networking has, for the most part, taken the place of traditional networking.

To do this, you must connect to the many SOCIAL MEDIA tools that will give you a direct link to all different kinds and sizes of companies and professional careers via computer before ever getting a chance for a one-on-one interview. Social media means any and everything dealing with connections via the Internet. The terms online, web searching, blogging, twittering, Facebook, and mySpace should be familiar to you if you want to compete in the job markets of the 21st century. This may put a frown on your face if you are stuck in "old school" methods of finding a job, but this is a means to actually applying for jobs and actually meeting someone that might otherwise be untouchable.

These various social media sites can be your gateway to other companies just merely by being linked to the many online sources as a way to introduce yourself, and, in addition, to connect and network with people you might not otherwise meet. This, in turn, could mean finding that perfect job. Job listings are posted on the Internet as well as their availability, so this way of searching for a job actually saves you from making many phone calls to see if they are hiring in your field.

Making a phone call to introduce yourself or faxing over your resume or even showing up at the front door are no longer acceptable methods of finding a job. In fact, this could actually hinder your chance of getting the job, because most companies expect the candidate for hire to have some knowledge of computers. By showing up to hand-deliver a resume, this might indicate otherwise. If you are not computer-literate or computer-savvy, the first step you would need to take is investing in a computer class, which can also be done online.

Unfortunately, the major downfall to social media and digital networking is that there is more access to companies, and therefore, the number of job applicants and competition increase. For this reason, having the picture-perfect resume that attracts a company becomes even more important in this day and age *(Refer to Chapter 3 on "Resume Writing")*.

Relying on Referrals

Earlier we talked about utilizing social media sites to meet people from all over the world who are also working in various industries. Connecting with someone and becoming a social media acquaintance could assist with your being hired if that person refers you for a particular position. Companies tend to look more carefully at referred candidates rather than sifting and filtering through a large stack of resumes to find the right candidate. Digital networking can do just that for you, but you must be in the social media game in order to play the game. For this reason, it is essential to have effective networking skills. This is the learning curve from the traditional way of looking for a job to the new social media methods of actually getting a job.

Increasing Networking Database

Social networking increases the number of people you might encounter on a day-to-day, month-to-month, and year-to-year timeline. Keep track of who you meet and where you've met them through the social network. This is a way of building your database, and becomes your little black book to your future career. For example, think about how many people you may meet in the day; that number can be from 0 to 10. Social media networking connections allow for meeting thousands of people around the world and in just one day. Consider the fact that each person is connected to a company that might be a potential job lead, and can actually walk your resume in and put it on the desk of the person hiring for the position you desire.

Connect to Social Media before Desperately Needing a Job

Social networking actually means being connected 24/7. You have to engage with people weekly and sometimes daily as new people connect with you online. This can be done while you are gainfully employed so that, if you're ever looking for a job, your network of acquaintances has already been established.

A Word of Caution

Remember when engaging in social networking and making it known that you are seeking employment, you are not alone. What you put on the Internet stays on the Internet and is available for many to see. Be aware that your boss or employers in your office will probably be socially connected as well. Be discreet, and if you meet a person that can connect you to a job, contact that person privately instead of through the worldwide network.

Face-to-face Contact

Although social networking is the venue to actually beginning a search for a job and to making contacts, there is still a need to have some face-to-face encounters. Usually certain professions and people in those professions will have social networking opportunities face-to-face. Or, meeting someone at a business before actually looking for a job could be beneficial in the long run because a face is now connected to that social media person.

Social Networking Leads to Face-to-Face

Even within your own company, you may be attending various social events or participating in various activities. If you're going to a convention or conference meeting and it is with companies that you might consider being employed with, research who will be attending through social networking prior to going. Let them know you are attending too and will introduce yourself. Now when you connect with them through your online source, you can remind them of where you met them. Now you've made a true connection using social media methods.

Connecting Social Media with Face-to-Face

Understanding how to use social media to your advantage and being able to research the many professional sites through connection links is important to finding a job or changing careers. In addition, social media networking can and does lead to a face-to-face encounter that enhances your chances of getting a job when you need it the most.

CHAPTER 27

It's Not Your Fault You Can't Re-Enter into the Job Market or Find a job

Can we always blame the U.S. President
for High Unemployment Rates?
Know how to keep yourself gainfully employed.

It's Not Your Fault

You Can't Re-Enter into the Job Market or Find a job

Can we always blame the U.S. President for High Unemployment Rates? Know how to keep yourself gainfully employed.

Should citizens always blame the President of the United States for high unemployment rates when they happen? There are some influences that can point directly to a president, but there are other key factors that dictate the rise or fall of unemployment possibilities in America.

As with any change in a government, citizens become concerned about employment. The uncertainty of it all is enough to make many worry, especially if citizens might still struggle with the political shift of power. However, economic factors, technology advancements, corporate values, and seasonal fluctuations are influential circumstances that determine the high or the low unemployment rate for the United States.

Any of these factors, as well as, former or future president relations and dealings with foreign relations and domestic affairs, can also play a role to determine if there will be jobs available to citizens…how many or how few. Nonetheless, it is important to understand the other components that can keep you working or not.

First, economic factors deal directly with national job growth. The economic climate determines if employees will stay on a job, or look for work that pays more if the employment industry seems to be a little more stable. Consequently, if there are too many available jobs, it may be hard for employers to keep a staff because there are an array of employment options. But on the other side of the spectrum, in a recession, most people tend to hold on to their current jobs until the market changes, thus an economic factor. In a recession, however, corporations may not be able to hold on to its employees due to the lack of revenue.

Technology advances are another factor that dictates if unemployment rates will fall or rise. Corporations are moving toward the most technological advancements, instead of relying on manpower. Therefore, it is advised to learn as many skills as possible in the high-tech industry in order to move right along with the changing face of corporations. For example, in the past, factory jobs needed humans to work the assembly line. Today, humans are being replaced with technology - robots and machines, to be exact. This decreases the number of "human" workers in the job market, creating a path for higher unemployment rates.

Third, bad press will quickly change the profile of a corporation, edging people away from applying for jobs at that company. Current employees will look for other opportunities to avoid reputation issues that might play a negative role with their efforts to find future work. If employees begin to resign, this could create a serious problem for the company. Closing of businesses and corporations will lead to a rise of unemployment rates.

Fourth, seasonal fluctuations occur every year, especially hitting the agriculture and construction industries. Employees may find that they are overwhelmed with a lot of work, or overwhelmed with not having any work, especially in construction. Summer is also a season that can be invaded with more job seekers during the time students leave school to work. Part-time jobs are hit the most, which helps the unemployment rate, until this flood of students quit and return back to school.

So why is all of this important enough to talk about? While the government can do its damage to increase the unemployment rate, it is not solely to blame when the other factors are considered. The question is what can you do about it? Be prepared. Always have your resume circulating. Let social media work for you while you are at work. Stay high-tech trained. Observe what companies require in your field of interest. Get an education. Seek to always improve your skills. Watch the job market trends, and make sure you evolve the same way. Reinvent yourself. Stay connected. Keep a door or two opened outside of your current job. Make smart career changes. Plan strategically, efficiently, and carefully.

Now that you know what factors play a role in determining if you are working or not, do something about it. Always look for a path that leads to open doors to keep you gainfully employed, and never give up!

Calvin L. Lovick, Publisher/Founder

Calvin Lovick is the Publisher/Founder of Lovick Minority Career Journal, an international employment publication. Lovick has 33 impressive years of experience in Corporate Human Resources Recruitment, 15 years in publishing and six years in Sports Event Planning.

Lovick Minority Career Journal is a quarterly publication with a circulation of 40,000 that provides comprehensive information and relevant articles about career opportunities in the Aerospace, Financial, Retail, Manufacturing and Technical industries.

Lovick also specializes in marketing, sales, advertising, and production coordination in addition to being a successful event planner and organizer. Having successfully conducted at least 30 Job Fairs/ Expos per year for the past 12 years, he was recognized by Fortune 500 companies in Southern California as a leader in helping to meet diversity recruitment goals in a cost-effective manner.

One of his prize events is the Silver Dollar Football Classic, an annual black college football-sporting event designed to bring awareness and recognition to over 100 Historically Black Colleges/Universities, whose contribution in education is helping to keep America strong. In addition to the two prominent football teams, this event also highlights their exhilarating, split-second precision marching bands equally competitive in the traditional Battle of the Bands.

Lovick is also the Senior Managing Partner of C.L. Lovick & Associates, which is billed as one of Southern California's premier Retained Executive Search firms.

He holds a Bachelor of Science degree in Business Management, Kean University, New Jersey - Class of '75. He served in the United States Air Force (1968-1971) with an Honorable Discharge.

Angela M. Cranon-Charles, M.A., Publisher/Editor-in-Chief

Angela M. Cranon-Charles has been the Publisher/Owner of Hollywood Scriptwriter Magazine (www.hollywoodscriptwriter.com) since 2003, and Co-Publisher and Editor-in-Chief of Lovick Minority Career Journal since 1991.

She holds a Masters of Arts degree in Science from California State University, Long Beach; a Bachelors of Arts degree in Journalism from San Diego State University; and a Professional Designation Journalism Certificate from the University of California, Los Angeles.

After earning her Journalism degree, she immediately began her professional journalism career as a reporter, anchor, and talk show host, working at prominent media outlets as ABC, CBS, the Financial News Network, Continental Cablevision, and Scripps Howard. She has earned numerous journalism honors and awards including, a Cable Diamond Award for "Best Community Event "Changing of the Guard: Police Chief Willie Williams," Alliance of Community Media Award for Best Local Newscast, and the Recognition Award for "Riot Coverage" from the Greater Los Angeles Press. Honors include Outstanding Young Women of America, The National Political Science Honor Society, and Phi Sigma Alpha Honor Society. She has extensive public speaking and talk-show host experience.

Since 1999, she has served as a professor for a number of colleges and universities nationwide. She is also a member of the Delta Sigma Theta sorority. *(Photo by Jeremiah Edward Charles)*

www.ingramcontent.com/pod-product-compliance
Lightning Source LLC
Chambersburg PA
CBHW030745180526
45163CB00003B/922